Sunset

Low-Cost Cookery

Great Meals at Real Savings

By the Editors of Sunset Books
and Sunset Magazine

Lane Publishing Co. • Menlo Park, California

Edited by Jerry Anne DiVecchio

Research and text: Holly Lyman

Design: JoAnn Masaoka

Illustrations: Alice Harth

Cover: Pork Pot Roast with Oranges, Pot-roasted
Onions and Potatoes (recipe on page 33).
Photographed by Darrow M. Watt.

Executive Editor, Sunset Books: David E. Clark

Second Printing March 1976. World rights reserved.
Copyright © Lane Publishing Co. Menlo Park, CA 94025.
Library of Congress No. 75-26488. SBN Title No. 376-02481-X.
Lithographed in the United States.

Contents

Special Features

Adventure in Economy

Audacity and realism—artfully combined to give the right perspective of economy in the kitchen—are the backbone of this book. A practical approach to food is basic to all *Sunset* cook books: how to get the best return for your effort. But in *Low-Cost Cookery*, we deal head-on with inflation and the uphill trend of food prices—though never at the sacrifice of eating well.

This book places prime importance on flavor interest. Recipes feature the less expensive main ingredients. The focus, instead of being on the higher priced loin sections of beef, veal, lamb, and pork, is on so-called "less tender" and correspondingly less costly cuts from shoulder, rump, shanks, breast, or brisket, as well as on preparation techniques for such lesser known items as squid, beef heart, or ground turkey. Also included is a wide spectrum of dishes based on ground meats and on other protein-rich ingredients such as eggs, cheese, and legumes. But we often call for judicious flavoring with spices, herbs, nuts, dried fruits, or seasonings—ingredients that are small extravagances, perhaps, but ones that give the dishes a special touch.

Starting with the festive meals in the opening chapter, this book continues throughout to draw heavily on international cuisines as inspiration for inexpensive main-dish recipes and an exciting array of menu ideas to accompany them. After all, peoples around the world have been developing low-cost cuisines for centuries;

now we can benefit from the variety of their experience.

You'll discover, as you leaf through the following pages, that the art of low-cost cookery depends a great deal on a sense of the dramatic. This book contains a pageant of food that is bright in color, subtle and unusual in taste combinations, and arresting in manner of presentation. The special treatment may be as simple as wrapping a frankfurter in a sauce-dipped tortilla, as cozy as making a meal of cheese melted before the fire, or as elegant as serving chicken breasts in an aureole of flaming liqueur.

ooo

Shopping Techniques. Planning combined with flexibility in the market keeps costs down when you shop. To help you take advantage of the best buys of the day, we provide relevant information throughout the book on seasonal shopping, buying in quantity when an item is on sale, substituting one meat or fish for another in a recipe in order to take advantage of a bargain price. Look for these hints where you see the symbol at right below.

ooo

The Respected Leftover. Leftovers are the treasure trove of the thrifty cook; we have included recipes in the book that are planned deliberately to produce extras for a second meal. We've also included a number of recipes that adapt themselves particularly well to the inclusion of leftovers.

Starting from scratch. Do-it-yourself basic preparation is another avenue of economy we investigate. It can take time—making your own yogurt, sprouting beans and seeds yourself, boning your own poultry—but the rewards are great in fun, flavor, and saving.

Consider this book a *workbook*. You can use the basic information it contains on ingredients and techniques to lay the groundwork for a cost-saving approach to cooking. Then turn to the variety of recipes—each distinctive in flavor, method of preparation, or manner of presentation —to gain a sense of the range of possibilities open to you as you develop your own unique style of low-cost cookery.

ooo

The Thrifty Kitchen. Conservation is a key word when it comes to keeping cooking costs down. Throughout the book we point up various ways to minimize waste and maximize use of *everything* that comes through your kitchen: saving bones to make broth; freezing orange peel to use for flavoring; letting potatoes share the oven with the roast; buying and preparing mushrooms in bulk for freezing. To make it easy to find such pieces of information (usually relating to some ingredient or technique in the recipes that precede them) we've marked them with the following symbol:

Festive Economy for Family and Friends

What quicker way to shake the notion that economy means dullness than to have a party for family or friends that proves just the opposite.

A fresh look at what makes a meal special is prerequisite. It's not the costliness of the ingredients but the style and imagination with which everyday foods are put together that makes these meals distinctive. Additionally, each of the eight menus in this chapter is served with showmanship and flair, in rather unconventional fashion: picnics to tote or to heat at the site (which may be no farther away than the patio); serve-yourself affairs where each person has great freedom in assembling a meal or seasoning a dish to suit precisely his or her taste; even a cook-it-yourself menu.

Ground beef is the star of the Mexican taco supper. Breads and flavorful butters are a lively and hearty extension of the English view of tea time. Grilled skewered meats from southeast Asia use such nonexotic ingredients as lean steak (but not a luxury cut) and peanut butter. A Japanese cook-as-you-eat meal lays tasteful emphasis on colorful, wholesome vegetables—as does the Lebanese *couscous* menu. One pot cookery is explored from Spanish and Nomadic points of view— and the results are surprisingly and deliciously unalike.

Picadillo Picnic

Ground beef served Mexican-style as *picadillo* (pih-cah-*dee*-oh) and served informally as the base for tacos makes a festive and simple meal for four to six. You can serve at home or on a picnic. Consider the menu, perhaps, as a birthday party dinner for youngsters; the informality of eating dinner out of hand makes serving easy to manage with a high spirited group.

Serve iced tea, orange juice, sangria, or Mexican beer to complement the cinnamon spiced meat filling; to end the meal, offer refreshing chunks of watermelon, or bananas to peel and eat.

> Picadillo (directions follow)
> Warm corn tortillas (directions follow)
> About 1½ cups shredded mild Cheddar cheese
> About 2 cups finely shredded iceberg lettuce
> 1 or 2 medium-size tomatoes, chopped
> 1 small onion, chopped
> 1 small package (3 oz.) cream cheese
> Guacamole (page 32) or 1 can (7 oz.) frozen avocado dip, thawed

To make tacos, divide picadillo evenly and spoon some down center of each warm tortilla; add some cheese, lettuce, tomato, onion, and cream cheese; add guacamole to taste; fold tortilla over filling and hold to eat, making sure the opposite end is held up so it won't drip. Makes 4 to 6 servings.

Picadillo. Thinly slice or crumble ¼ pound chorizo sausage (optional) and combine in a frying pan with 1 pound lean ground beef (if chorizo is omitted, increase beef to 1¼ lb.), 1 chopped medium-size onion, and ¼ teaspoon ground cinnamon. Cook, stirring, until meat begins to brown. Add ¼ cup raisins, 1 can (4½ oz.) chopped ripe olives, ½ cup catsup, and ½ cup water.

Simmer uncovered, stirring occasionally, until most of the liquid is evaporated. Serve hot; or make ahead, chill, and reheat.

Warm corn tortillas. Place a frying pan over medium heat. Dip your hands in water and then rub over the surface of a corn tortilla. Drop tortilla into hot pan and flip over every few seconds until it is soft and warm and the surface puffs slightly. Transfer at once to a tightly covered container or an envelope made of foil and keep in a warm place while you heat each additional tortilla; stack together. Well-wrapped tortillas stay hot several hours. Allow 2 or 3 tortillas for each serving.

A Bread and Butter Party

When you present this lively and light-hearted adaptation of the English tradition of high tea, be sure your guests know it's going to be a full-meal occasion.

Featured are a handsome variety of breads and some specially flavored butters, supplemented by an assortment of cheese and baskets of vegetables and fruit. Include jug wine or jugs of fruit juice and ample coffee.

You can easily adjust the scale of the party to any size group, and once arranged colorfully on a table—or several tables, depending on the amount—the food requires no tending.

If you like to bake, now is the time to show off your skills and take the economic advantages of doing it yourself. If time is short, you can buy the breads. Either way, breads can be held in the freezer until party time.

Basket of breads

Allow the equivalent of a 1-pound loaf for every 4 or 5 guests. Choose (or bake) breads that offer contrasts in: *size*—whole loaves, individual rolls; *flavor*—white, whole grain, sweet, sour, savory; *texture*—crisp, crusty, tender, chewy.

Among possible choices: Armenian cracker bread, Scandinavian crisp bread, dense pumpernickels, golden egg breads, raisin bread, long crusty baguettes, plump sourdough loaves, Arab pocket bread, finger-size rolls, bagels, onion rolls.

Keep breads whole to preserve their freshness.

Provide a large board and knife at the table, so each person can cut bread as desired.

Flavored butters

You can make up the butters 2 or 3 days in advance and keep, covered, in the refrigerator. Set the pots of butter around the basket of breads; label pots so guests will know which is which, as some are sweet and some are savory. A total of 2 pounds of butter, seasoned as follows, makes enough for about 20 servings; you can cut recipes in half, if desired. (Leftovers are good with toast or in sandwiches.)

Red onion butter. In a small pan boil ¼ cup wine vinegar with ½ cup minced red onion and ½ teaspoon tarragon leaves, stirring, until liquid is evaporated. Let cool; then blend with 1 cup (½ lb.) soft butter or margarine and ¼ cup minced parsley. Makes about 1½ cups.

Beefy butter. Smoothly blend 1 cup (½ lb.) soft butter or margarine with 1 or 2 teaspoons (to taste) meat sauce extract or beef stock concentrate. Makes 1 cup.

Moroccan apple date butter. Mix ½ cup finely chopped tart apple (peeled) with 1 tablespoon lemon juice, ¼ teaspoon ground cinnamon, 2 tablespoons brown sugar, and ½ cup finely chopped pitted dates. Blend into 1 cup (½ lb.) soft butter or margarine. Makes about 2 cups.

Honey butter. Blend 3 tablespoons honey with 1 cup (½ lb.) butter or margarine. Makes 1 cup.

Cheese board

Allow about ¼ pound for each person, but keep cheese pieces whole so they don't dry out. Let guests cut their own. You might have whole colby cheese or baby Edam, a chunk of jack or Swiss cheese, cream cheese, Camembert, Brie, as you like. Leftovers can be used later.

Vegetables in ice

Put ice in the bottom of a suitable size container and pile on top ready-to-eat green onions, slender carrots, celery stalks, and radishes; allow 2 or 3 vegetables per person.

Fruit basket

Choose easy-to-handle fruits such as whole strawberries, oranges, bananas, apples, pears, grapes; 1 whole fruit or 3 or 4 berries make a serving.

Salad Sandwich Supper

A buffet of boldly flavored salads, to eat as salads or as sandwich fillings, is the starting point for this relaxed entertainment.

To serve eight, you'll want to make all four of the salads: chicken, tuna, mushroom, and ratatouille (rah-tah-*too*-ee)—and this can be done at least a day in advance. You may find any individual salad just the answer for a meal for two.

You'll need a 1-pound loaf of French or sourdough bread (regular loaf or long, skinny baguettes) for each 4 servings; split loaf lengthwise and butter the cut surfaces.

Also include a bowl of washed and crisped lettuce leaves (1 large head butter lettuce or red leaf lettuce for 6 to 8 servings) for the sandwiches or to put on serving plates and top with salad. An optional addition is a tray of thinly sliced cooked ham and Swiss cheese, also to add to sandwiches.

Let guests help themselves at their own pace, making up several sandwiches or just having bread and butter as they try all the salads.

Serve chilled white wine or iced tea. For dessert, offer fruit—berries with cream, sliced melon, honey and peaches; or make an apple pie (page 90).

Curried chicken salad. Blend together ½ cup mayonnaise, ½ teaspoon garlic salt, 1 teaspoon curry powder, ⅛ teaspoon cayenne, ½ teaspoon prepared mustard, 2 teaspoons lemon juice, and 2 tablespoons finely chopped Major Grey's chutney. Add 3½ cups cold cooked (skinned and boned) chicken, cut in about ½-inch chunks, ⅔ cup thinly sliced celery, 2 thinly sliced green onions (tops included), and 1 small apple (diced); stir to blend. Cover and chill if made ahead. Just before serving sprinkle with 3 tablespoons chopped salted almonds. Makes 4½ cups.

Tuna salad. Stir together 1 cup tomato-based chile sauce, ¼ cup lemon juice, 2 cloves garlic (minced or pressed), 1 teaspoon basil leaves, and 2 teaspoons prepared horseradish. Add 1 small onion (chopped) and ½ cup whole pitted ripe olives. Cover and chill if made ahead. Just before serving add 2 cans (about 7 oz. *each*) tuna (including oil) and mix gently together just until tuna is lightly coated with sauce.

Garnish top with several peperoncini (Italian pickled peppers), if desired. Makes 4 cups.

Marinated mushroom salad. Wash and trim ends from 1¼ pounds small mushrooms (or quarter medium-size mushrooms). Place in boiling salted water to cover; simmer, uncovered, 5 minutes. Drain and let cool.

Mix together 6 tablespoons olive oil, 2 tablespoons lemon juice, 1 clove garlic (minced or pressed), ½ teaspoon *each* crushed whole black pepper, whole coriander seed, whole mustard seed, and salt. Add mushrooms, 1 small onion (finely chopped), and ½ cup minced parsley; stir to blend. Cover and chill, stirring occasionally, for at least 2 hours. Makes 3½ cups.

Ratatouille salad. In a large frying pan saute 1 medium-size onion (finely chopped) and 1 clove garlic (minced or pressed) in 3 tablespoons olive oil until limp. Add 1 small (about ¾ lb.) eggplant (cut in 1-inch cubes), 1 medium-size zucchini (cut in ½-inch-thick slices), 1 medium-size green pepper (cut in ¼-inch strips), ¼ cup chopped parsley, 1 can (1 lb.) pear-shaped tomatoes (including liquid), 1 teaspoon *each* basil leaves and salt.

Break tomatoes into small pieces with a spoon. Cover and simmer, stirring occasionally, until all vegetables are tender (about 30 minutes). Cook, uncovered, stirring occasionally, over high heat until most of the liquid has evaporated; stir to prevent sticking. (Cool, cover, and chill if made ahead.) Serve hot or cold with about ⅓ cup grated Parmesan cheese to sprinkle over individual servings. Makes 4 cups.

Satay on a Stick

Satay are mini-shish kebabs from Malaysia, Singapore, and Indonesia. Bite-size bits of marinated meat are threaded on slender wooden skewers, then barbecued or broiled, and finally swirled through a lively peanut sauce.

You pull each bite from the skewer with your teeth, then also use the skewer to spear, between bites of meat, the pressed rice cubes and marinated cucumber salad.

If it's an outdoor party, you can even let the guests cook their own satay. A basket of tropical fruits—pineapple, papaya, mango, banana—is an ideal way to end this meal.

The economical flexibility of satay comes from the meat choices. You can use either beef, lamb, or chicken, or a combination—according to taste and best buy of the day.

   3 pounds lean boneless meat—top round or sirloin of beef; shoulder or leg of lamb; or chicken (see How to Bone Chicken, page 50)
   2 tablespoons curry powder
  ½ cup *each* salad oil and soy sauce
   4 cloves garlic, minced or pressed
   2 tablespoons sugar
      Peanut sauce (recipe follows)
      Pressed rice cubes (recipe follows)
      Marinated cucumber and onion salad (recipe follows)

Cut meat in ¾-inch cubes; if using more than one kind of meat, keep each separate.

Stir together curry powder, oil, soy, garlic, and sugar. Pour over meat; if you use more than one kind of meat, put each in a separate plastic bag and set together in a bowl. Add an equal amount of marinade to each. Cover and chill at least 4 hours or up to 2 days.

String meat on long bamboo skewers (about 12-inch size), filling each skewer about halfway up; you need enough skewer exposed to hold while eating and cooking. If using different meats, thread each kind onto separate skewers.

To barbecue, arrange skewered meats on a platter alongside the fire. One person can cook all the satay, adding to grill as needed, or people can tend satay individually. Place on a grill 2 inches above a solid bed of completely ignited coals. Turn frequently until meat is browned to your liking (takes 8 to 10 minutes).

To broil, arrange satay slightly apart on a rack in broiler pan. Broil about 3 inches from heat, turning to brown evenly (takes 8 to 10 minutes).

Swish satay through peanut sauce and then slide a bite of meat off skewer with your teeth to eat. Use skewer to spear rice cubes and marinated cucumber and onion salad to eat along with satay. (Or you can serve these foods on a plate to eat with a fork.) Makes 8 to 9 servings.

Peanut sauce. Whirl 1 cup salted Virginia peanuts in a blender until finely ground; remove from blender and set aside.

Whirl 1 large onion (cut in chunks), 2 cloves garlic, and 4 or 5 small, dried hot red peppers in blender until smooth. Pour 2 tablespoons salad oil into a frying pan and place over medium heat. Add onion mixture, 2 teaspoons ground coriander, 1 teaspoon ground cumin seed; cook, stirring occasionally, for 5 minutes. Reduce heat to low, add ground peanuts, then gradually stir in 1 can (12 oz.) thawed frozen coconut milk (or use milk and coconut alternative that follows), 3 tablespoons brown sugar, 2 tablespoons *each* lemon juice and soy sauce. Cook, uncovered, just below simmering (do not boil), stirring occasionally, until sauce thickens (about 15 minutes).

Serve warm or at room temperature in wide, shallow, rimmed dishes; for serving convenience, use 2 or 3 dishes. If made a day ahead, cool, cover, and chill; to serve, stir over low heat, just until warmed through. Makes 2½ cups.

(If you can't buy frozen coconut milk, whirl 1 cup milk with ½ cup shredded coconut in blender; pour through wire strainer and use liquid.)

Pressed rice cubes. In a pan combine 1½ cups pearl or other short grain rice and 2½ cups water. Bring to a boil, cover, and simmer 25 minutes or just until water is absorbed. Pour hot rice into a 9-inch square pan and, with the back of a metal spoon or wide spatula (rinse with water to prevent sticking), press rice down very firmly to form an even layer. Cool thoroughly. If you do this a day ahead, cover and chill.

Run a knife around edge of pan and turn rice out onto a board. Cut in 1-inch squares, rinsing knife frequently. Arrange on platter. Serve at room temperature. Makes 6 to 8 servings.

Marinated cucumber and onion salad. Cut 3 medium-size cucumbers in half lengthwise and then cut into crosswise slices about ¼ inch thick. Also cut 2 small red onions in half lengthwise, then in ¼-inch-thick crosswise slices. Stir together ½ teaspoon salt and 4 tablespoons *each* sugar and white wine vinegar; add cucumber and onion and mix gently together. Cover and chill up to 2 hours before serving. Makes 6 to 8 servings.

Mizutaki—a Cooperative Affair

Dinner cooked at the table is a friendly and festive way to entertain, and it's also easy on the hostess. One of the most colorful meals of this type is the Japanese peasant dish, *mizutaki* (me-zoo-*tah*-key).

As you are seated, a simmering container of hot broth awaits the addition of meat, fish, vegetables from carefully arranged trays. Mizutaki serves six, the maximum number that a table can comfortably accommodate. If you want to serve more, duplicate the service on another table.

The cooker may be as simple as an electric frying pan, which works very well. But the classic utensil for mizutaki is a charcoal fired metal pot with center chimney, and around the chimney a moat that holds the broth. Several cautions when using the cooker—fill the moat with liquid before igniting coals; have adequate ventilation (set the cooker outdoors or in the fireplace when you set the coals on fire); protect your table by setting the cooker in a low rimmed dish (such as a large flower pot saucer) filled with water—otherwise the hot ash dropping to the bottom of the cooker will damage your table.

The host or hostess can add the first batch of foods to cook, or each person can add foods of his or her choice to the simmering broth. Everyone has a bowl of rice and dipping sauce, and as foods are cooked, you pluck them out bite by bite with chopsticks, dip in sauce, and eat with rice.

When all the foods are cooked, you ladle the now greatly enriched cooking broth into the remainder of the sauce and sip as a soup.

2 pounds lean boneless meat—beef flank or top round steak, chicken, shoulder or leg of lamb, or pork loin end or shoulder
  About 1 pound (1 bunch) spinach
  Water
6 carrots, thinly sliced
1 small head cauliflower, cut into small flowerets
12 green onions, cut in 2-inch lengths (include some tops)
½ pound mushrooms, thinly sliced
½ pound tofu (see Tofu, page 79), cut in ½-inch cubes
  About 2 quarts regular-strength chicken broth
  Mizutaki sauce (directions follow)
6 to 8 cups hot cooked rice

Cut meat in about ⅛-inch-thick slices; cut all slices into pieces no bigger than about 1½-inch squares. If you use more than one kind, keep each separate. Break tender leaves from spinach into a quantity of water; wash and drain well several times.

On a wide tray (or several smaller ones) carefully arrange each food separately and side by side, alternating colors for most effective presentation: meat, spinach leaves, carrots, cauliflower, onions, mushrooms, and tofu (if you don't plan to serve right away, keep tofu separate—it drains). You can cover and chill foods for several hours.

About 30 minutes before time to eat, place electric frying pan in center of serving table (or cooker; see preceding cautions) with broth (no more than ⅔ full). When broth is simmering; bring to table the trays of food, and at each place have a bowl of hot rice, a bowl of mizutaki sauce, chopsticks (or tongs), and a soup spoon.

Invite guests to be seated. Add about half the foods to simmering broth, keeping each kind separate (or ask each person to choose a section of the cooker to add foods to). Cover and let return to simmer; then cook about 5 minutes. Remove lid and eat morsels, a bite at a time, transferring from broth to sauce to rice. When all is eaten, add remaining food; cover, cook, and eat as before. Turn off electric pan or snuff coals. Ladle some of the hot broth into each cup of sauce and sip. (If using charcoal cooker, add water to moat if you have served all the broth—and coals are still hot.) Makes 6 servings.

Mizutaki sauce. In a blender whirl 1 egg with 2 tablespoons wine vinegar and ¼ teaspoon dry mustard; at high speed, gradually but steadily add 1 cup salad oil. Scoop sauce into a bowl and blend in ⅓ cup sour cream, 2 tablespoons soy sauce, 2 tablespoons Sherry or Marin (rice wine), and

⅓ cup regular-strength chicken or beef broth. Cover and chill until ready to use. Divide equally among 6 small dishes.

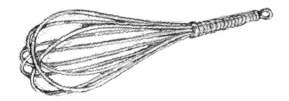

Nomad One-pot Picnic

Suited perfectly to picnicking as so few utensils are required for heating and eating, this meal can also be interestingly adapted to a barbecue on the patio or the fireplace. It features a series of treats, Middle Eastern in style and flavor, that come from one pot.

Meatballs, made earlier, are reheated in broth, giving the broth a bonus of good tastes. The broth is drawn off to serve as a sipping soup, and cooked pilaf is added to the meat for warming. This mixture is spooned into the hollow of Arab pocket bread (also called Arabic, Armenian, pita, peta, or peeta bread), relishes are added, and the meal is eaten as a sandwich. (If pocket bread is not available, you can use flour tortillas; heat as directed in the picadillo recipe on page 7.) Tangerines or oranges, dates, and, if available, Middle Eastern cookies or pastries arranged on a tray make a pretty dessert.

> 1 large can (47 oz.) or 6 cups regular-strength chicken broth
>   Spiced meatballs (directions follow)
> 2 lemons, cut in wedges
>   Pilaf (directions follow)
> 8 to 16 rounds of Arab pocket bread (or 8 to 16 flour tortillas)
> 1 head romaine, washed, drained, and chilled
> 3 or 4 tomatoes, cut in wedges
> 2 or 3 green peppers, seeded and cut in strips
>   Green onion yogurt sauce (directions follow)

Pour broth into a 5 to 6-quart kettle and bring to a boil (on a small campfire, on a barbecue, pushed close to the fire in a fireplace—or even on the kitchen range). Add spiced meatballs and return to simmer.

Holding meat back with a spoon, pour hot broth into a pitcher or kettle with a spout.

Serve cups of hot broth, adding lemon juice to taste, while rest of meal is being prepared.

Add pilaf to meatballs and stir until heated.

Tear a round of Arab bread in half crosswise to make half-moon; spoon meat and rice into pocket of bread, adding romaine, tomatoes, green pepper, and green onion yogurt sauce to taste. Repeat to make each serving. Makes 8 to 10 servings.

Spiced meatballs. Mince 3 medium-size onions and cook in 4 tablespoons butter, margarine, or olive oil, stirring until soft. Pour into a large bowl and add 3 pounds lean ground lamb or beef, 2 teaspoons salt, 1½ teaspoons ground cumin seed, ¾ teaspoon ground cinnamon, ½ teaspoon pepper, ½ cup fine dry bread crumbs, ½ cup milk, and 2 eggs. Mix very well.

Shape meat into 1-inch-diameter balls and place just slightly apart on rimmed baking sheets. Bake in a 450° oven for 20 minutes or until browned; if you bake two pans at once, alternate their rack positions about halfway through the baking. Cool meat thoroughly and keep cold, covered, until ready to reheat in broth.

Pilaf. Heat ⅓ cup butter, margarine, or olive oil in a wide frying pan; add ⅓ cup pine nuts or slivered blanched almonds and cook on moderate heat, stirring, just until nuts are golden; remove at once from pan with a slotted spoon and set aside.

To butter in frying pan add 2 medium-size onions, finely chopped, and cook, stirring, over medium heat until soft but not browned. Add 1 cup pearl rice and continue to cook on moderate heat, stirring, until rice turns opaque. Pour in 2 cups regular-strength chicken broth and add a 2 or 3-inch cinnamon stick, 1 teaspoon mustard seed, ¼ teaspoon coriander seed, and 2 whole cloves. Bring to a boil, cover, reduce heat to simmer, and cook 15 to 20 minutes, stirring occasionally, until liquid is absorbed and rice is tender. Cool; add nuts and then chill, covered, until ready to reheat.

Green onion yogurt sauce. Blend 1 cup minced green onions (including some tops), 2 cups unflavored yogurt, and salt to taste. Cover and chill until ready to serve. Makes 3 cups.

Lamb and Pea Couscous

Around the eastern and southern shores of the Mediterranean, *couscous* (koos-koos) is served often and in a wide variety of ways. Usually it's a main dish, and usually it's based on a special pastalike preparation of wheat (known also as couscous), but frequently other grains or legumes are used instead.

(Recipe continued on next page)

In this Lebanese couscous, a whole festive dinner revolves around a central dish of lamb and split peas, simmered together in a spicy broth.

Couscous makes an entertainment for about eight people. You can present the meal at a table, but it's livelier when you group all the couscous dishes on a large tray and then seat your guests around it on a rug on the floor or ground.

The simple dishes that accompany a couscous can be made early in the day. Serve the meal with plenty of Arab pocket bread, fresh fruit, and perhaps some flaky baklava pastry.

2 tablespoons olive oil or salad oil
3 pounds boneless lamb stew, cut in about 1½-inch cubes
2 large onions, chopped
¼ cup chopped coriander (or 2 tablespoons dried coriander)
2 teaspoons coriander seed, slightly crushed
1 teaspoon salt
1 teaspoon fennel seed
¼ teaspoon ground ginger
1 can (about 14 oz.) or 1¾ cups regular-strength chicken broth
  Water
1 package (12 oz. or 1¾ cups) split peas
  Coriander leaves
  About 2 cups unflavored yogurt
  Baked eggplant (directions follow)
  Sauteed zucchini (directions follow)
  Tabouli (directions follow)
  Hummus (directions follow)

Pour oil into 5 to 6-quart kettle. Add meat and brown on medium-high heat; set aside. Add onions, chopped coriander, coriander seed, salt, fennel seed, and ginger to oil. Cook and stir until onion is slightly browned. Return meat and any juices to pan. Combine broth with enough water to make 4½ cups liquid; add to meat. Bring stew to a boil, cover, and simmer gently 45 minutes (this much can be done a day ahead; cover and chill; reheat to continue cooking).

Meanwhile sort through peas and discard any extraneous materials; rinse and drain peas. Tie peas very loosely in a bag formed from washed cheesecloth (peas will double in volume).

After the meat has cooked the 45 minutes, make a well in the center of the pan and place in it the bag of peas, pushing down so liquid covers. Return to boil, then reduce heat to simmering. Check occasionally, and slightly turn bag so all the peas are in the liquid some of the time. Cook about 45 minutes more or until meat is very tender and peas mash easily. Pour peas from cloth into the center of a serving platter; press juices from cloth and pour onto peas. Surround with meat. Spoon balance of juice over meat. Garnish with coriander leaves. Accompany with containers of yogurt, baked eggplant, sauteed zucchini, hummus, and tabouli. Makes 8 to 10 servings.

Baked eggplant. Cut 1 large (about 1½ lb.) eggplant in half lengthwise, then cut crosswise in ½-inch-thick slices. Pour 6 to 7 tablespoons olive oil or salad oil into a rimmed baking sheet; turn eggplant in oil, coating all sides, and arrange in a single layer. Bake in a 450° oven for 35 to 40 minutes or until eggplant is browned and very soft when pressed. Serve at room temperature.

Sauteed zucchini. Cut about 1 pound zucchini (ends trimmed off) in ¼-inch-thick slices. Cook over medium-high heat in a wide frying pan with 2 tablespoons olive oil or salad oil, turning with a spatula, until zucchini is lightly browned (takes 8 to 10 minutes). Season with salt and spoon into a serving dish. Serve at room temperature; squeeze lemon juice onto servings.

Tabouli. Rinse ½ cup bulgur wheat several times; then combine with ½ cup cold water and let stand 1 hour; drain off any remaining liquid. Combine bulgur wheat with ½ cup minced parsley, ½ cup minced fresh mint or crumbled dried mint, 1 cup finely chopped green onions (including some tops), 1 large peeled and chopped tomato, 4 tablespoons olive oil or salad oil, 4 tablespoons lemon juice, and salt to taste. Cover and chill until ready to serve. Arrange tabouli in a mound and surround with small inner leaves of romaine lettuce; scoop up tabouli onto romaine to eat, if you like.

Hummus. Discard liquid from 1 can (1 lb.) garbanzos. Place garbanzos in a blender and add ½ cup chopped parsley, 2 cloves garlic, 2 tablespoons olive oil or salad oil, 3 tablespoons *each* lemon juice and whipping cream. Cover and whirl smooth. Chill, covered. To serve, mound in a bowl and garnish with 2 to 4 tablespoons finely chopped canned pimentos.

Peel and slice 2 large turnips; or peel and slice 1 cucumber. Tuck vegetable slices around hummus. To eat, scoop up hummus with vegetables.

Cocido in Three Courses

One of the oldest and most traditional Spanish meals is a simmered one-pot dinner called *cocido* (koh-*chee*-doh)—a selection of meats and vegetables that cook together in a savory broth, each ingredient contributing flavors to the whole.

Like many dishes from humble peasant origins, this cocido is basically thrifty despite its scale.

The way in which cocido is served turns it into a three course party meal. The cooking broth makes a delicious soup to begin the dinner; then the vegetables are served with one sauce, followed by (or consecutively presented with) a platter of the meats and the two sauces that go with them.

Just before the guests arrive, take meats and vegetables out of the pot, arrange on serving platters, and place in a warm oven.

With the soup, you might serve crusty French bread and dry white wine. A hearty dry red wine goes well with the meat course.

1 cup (about ½ lb.) dried garbanzos
  Water
3 tablespoons olive oil or salad oil
  3-pound broiler-fryer chicken, quartered
  About 1 pound kielbasa, linguisa, or garlic sausages
  About 2-pound piece fresh beef brisket
1 large onion, chopped
2 cloves garlic, minced or pressed
  About 1 pound smoked ham shank, quartered
4 cups regular-strength chicken or beef broth
2 bay leaves
  About ⅓ cup coarsely chopped parsley
8 medium-size carrots
¾ pound green beans
1 large (about 1½ lb.) cabbage, cut into 8 wedges
3 ounces thin pasta such as vermicelli or capellini, broken into 2-inch lengths
  Creamy mint sauce (recipe follows)
  Spicy tomato-cumin relish (recipe follows)
  Garlic sour cream sauce (recipe follows)

Rinse garbanzos; in a small pan, cover them with 3½ cups water. Bring to a boil, cover, and boil gently 5 minutes; remove from heat and let stand at least 1 hour.

In a kettle (at least 8 qt.) over medium heat, add oil. Add chicken quarters and deeply brown on all sides; remove from pan. Brown sausages on all sides and remove from pan.

In same pan, deeply brown beef brisket on all sides; then push to one side of pan. Add onion and garlic; cook, stirring, until onion is limp. Add ham shank, broth, bay leaves, parsley, garbanzos with their soaking liquid, and an additional 1 cup water. Bring to a boil, reduce heat, cover, and simmer 1½ hours.

Add browned chicken; cover and simmer 20 minutes. (If you like you can chill cocido over-night; lift off hard fat and discard; then reheat to simmer. Sausages should be chilled also.) Skim off and discard fat. Add carrots, green beans, and browned sausages; simmer 15 minutes or until vegetables are just tender when pierced with a fork.

While vegetables are cooking, bring about 3 quarts of water to a boil in a kettle. Add cabbage wedges and cook, uncovered, for 5 minutes or until tender and bright green; drain, saving cabbage water.

Transfer carrots, green beans, and garbanzos to a heatproof serving platter and arrange cabbage around other vegetables; cover. Remove meats and chicken from kettle and arrange on a second heatproof platter; cover. Place both platters in a warm oven until serving time (up to 1½ hours).

Pour cooking broth through a wire strainer and then combine with enough reserved cabbage cooking water to make 12 cups broth. Bring to a boil, add pasta, and boil for 5 minutes or until noodles are just tender.

Serve soup first; then offer vegetable platter with creamy mint sauce. Serve meat platter with vegetables or as a separate course. Pass tomato-cumin relish and garlic sour cream sauce, suggesting that guests blend them to eat with meats. Makes 12 servings.

Creamy mint sauce. In a blender combine 2 egg yolks, 1 tablespoon white wine vinegar, 1 teaspoon sugar, ⅛ teaspoon salt, and ½ cup finely chopped fresh mint leaves (or 2 tablespoons dried mint and 1 tablespoon water); whirl until smooth and slightly thickened. With blender on lowest speed, gradually pour in ½ cup (¼ lb.) melted butter or margarine and ⅓ cup whipping cream, whirling until smooth. Serve at room temperature. Cover and chill if made ahead.

Tomato-cumin relish. In a pan heat 2 tablespoons olive oil or salad oil; add 1 large onion (chopped), 1 large green pepper (seeded and chopped), and 1 clove garlic (minced or pressed). Cook, stirring, until onion is limp. Add 1 can (about 1 lb.) tomato sauce with tomato bits, ⅓ cup regular-strength chicken or beef broth (or water), 2 tablespoons lemon juice, ½ teaspoon *each* salt and basil leaves, and 1 teaspoon *each* sugar, ground cumin, and crushed hot red pepper. Cook, stirring, over medium heat until sauce thickens (about 10 minutes). Serve at room temperature. If made ahead, cover and chill.

Garlic sour cream sauce. In a small bowl smoothly blend ½ cup *each* sour cream and mayonnaise, 3 to 5 cloves garlic (minced or pressed), ½ teaspoon *each* lemon juice and salt, and ¼ teaspoon pepper. Cover and chill.

Thrifty Elegance with Beef

The challenge of turning the more economical cuts of beef into good-tasting dishes is well met in this chapter. Many an inspiration—for flavoring and for method of cooking or presentation—is borrowed from cooks abroad, who've dealt with the high cost of meat for centuries. From Italy, you'll find shanks braised in garlic sauce; from Scandinavia, a brisket of beef simmered tender with a garden display of vegetables; from South Africa, meat loaf with subtleties of fruit and spice; and from the Orient, a close look at the stir-fry technique, which makes a little meat seem like more.

You'll also come across many suggestions for making wiser choices when you shop. Steaks and roasts don't have to come from the expensive rib and loin of beef—there are many other possibilities when you know what to ask for.

Oxbringa

Oxbringa makes an easy-to-manage entree at a party for about a dozen guests—or you can plan deliberately for two meals, each to serve six, when you start this colorful Swedish boiled dinner.

The first night presentation is the slowly simmered beef surrounded by a garden display of vegetables that cook in the meat broth. The unifying touch is a creamy horseradish sauce made from the same broth. A green salad is a nice addition to the menu. For dessert consider fruit and cheese.

The next night or so, all that is left—meat, vegetables, sauce—gets turned into a satisfying main dish soup; you need to add canned or homemade broth.

5 to 5½-pound piece fresh lean beef brisket
1 large onion, chopped
1 large carrot, chopped
6 cups water
1 bay leaf
6 whole black peppers
1½ teaspoons salt
1 tablespoon *each* celery seed and mustard seed
12 to 24 red-skinned new potatoes, unpeeled (about 1 inch in diameter)
12 to 24 small white boiling onions (about 1 inch in diameter)
5 to 6 dozen assorted garden vegetables (suggestions follow)
¾ cup whipping cream
3 tablespoons cornstarch
Prepared horseradish

Trim excess fat from meat. Without adding fat, deeply brown meat in a large (about 8 qt.) heavy kettle; this is a large cut and will probably require shifting about in the pan to brown all surfaces. Lift out and set aside. Add the 1 large onion and carrot to the drippings and cook, stirring, until they are browned. Return meat to pan with the water, bay leaf, peppers, salt, celery seed, and mustard seed. Cover and simmer gently for about 2½ hours or until meat pierces easily. (This much can be done ahead; cover and refrigerate.)

Skim off and discard fat from broth. (If chilled, lift off solidified fat; reheat meat in stock until hot through, 35 to 45 minutes.) Transfer hot meat to a serving platter; keep warm. Pour broth through a wire strainer; discard seasoning vegetables and spices.

Heat the broth to a boil, add potatoes and onions, and simmer, covered, for about 15 minutes or until vegetables are tender when pierced; lift out with a slotted spoon and arrange around meat; keep warm. Add to broth your choice of the garden vegetables suggested and simmer, covered, for about 5 minutes or until just tender when pierced. Lift out with a slotted spoon and arrange around meat.

Blend cream with the cornstarch, add 2 tablespoons horseradish, and stir into broth; cook, stirring, until boiling and thickened. Pass gravy in a separate bowl to spoon over meat and vegetables. Also pass additional horseradish at the table. Makes about 12 servings, or 6 servings for one meal with leftovers for 6 servings as Oxbringa Soup (follows).

Garden vegetables. Choose at least 3 kinds from the following vegetables: small whole (about 3 inches long) carrots, green beans, parsnips, crookneck squash, zucchini, whole (1 to 1½-inch) patty pan squash, or turnips. If you buy larger market vegetables, just cut them to similar-size pieces.

Oxbringa Soup. This is phase two of oxbringa, if the first meal was for six.

Bring to boiling 3 cans (14 oz. *each*) or 6 cups regular-strength beef broth in a 4 to 5-quart kettle over high heat. Add leftover meat and vegetables from oxbringa (preceding), cut in bite-size pieces (you should have about 5 cups meat and 6 to 8 cups vegetables) and any leftover gravy. Season to taste with salt and pepper and heat through.

Just before serving, stir into the soup about ¼ cup *each* minced parsley and thinly sliced green onion; pass sour cream (about 1 cup) at the table to spoon into individual dishes. Makes 6 servings.

Try Second-time-around Dishes

Some roasts offer such delicious possibilities for using cooked meat in a second meal that it pays to cook twice as much as you need. Here are only a few of many possibilities: roast corned beef to slice cold for a sandwich meal, pot roast leftovers to turn into meat pies, baked fresh beef brisket to slice and reheat in the pan sauces, ham to grind for ham loaf, and cold roast turkey for salad.

Baked Brisket with Pan Sauce

It's the long, slow baking that turns this economical beef brisket into a tender, tasty roast. Leftovers can be reheated in the pan sauce or served cold.

(Recipe continued on next page)

6 to 7-pound piece well-trimmed fresh beef
brisket

⅓ cup *each* lemon juice and firmly packed
brown sugar

½ cup catsup

1 tablespoon Dijon or brown mustard

3 tablespoons Worcestershire

1 teaspoon salt

2 tablespoons *each* cornstarch and water

Lay meat flat in a baking pan with a rim higher than the surface of the meat. Blend lemon juice, sugar, catsup, mustard, Worcestershire, and salt; pour over meat.

Cover pan and bake in a 300° oven for 6 hours. If you cover pan with foil, make a cap of it so meat and foil will not touch; as the meat cooks it shrinks in length but gets thicker in the middle. (The acid in the sauce may cause foil to corrode.)

After 6 hours remove cover and bake another 1 to 1½ hours, basting frequently with juices, until meat pierces readily. Transfer meat to a carving board and keep warm. Skim off and discard fat from pan juices. Bring juices to a boil; blend cornstarch and water to a smooth paste and gradually stir into boiling sauce until it is of desired consistency (amount required depends upon quantity of pan juices developed during baking). Slice brisket thinly; spoon sauce over individual portions. Serve thinly sliced leftovers cold, or reheat in any remaining pan sauce. Makes 14 to 16 servings.

Fruit and Spice Pot Roast

Cranberries give a sweet-tart tang to chuck roast. Baked sweet potatoes or yams are good with the meat and gravy.

3 tablespoons all-purpose flour

1 teaspoon onion salt

½ teaspoon basil leaves

¼ teaspoon pepper

4¼ to 5-pound beef chuck roast

2 tablespoons salad oil

6 whole cloves

3-inch cinnamon stick or ½ teaspoon ground
cinnamon

Water

1 can (1 lb.) whole cranberry sauce

2 tablespoons lemon juice

Combine flour, salt, basil, and pepper; rub evenly over all sides of the roast, shaking off and saving any excess. Heat oil in a 4 to 5-quart kettle over medium heat; add roast; brown well on all sides. Add cloves, cinnamon, and ⅓ cup water; cover and simmer for 2 hours.

Stir in the cranberry sauce and lemon juice; continue to cook, covered, for about 30 minutes longer or until meat is tender when pierced. Lift meat to a warm serving platter; keep warm. Skim fat from pan juices. Blend remaining seasoned flour with an equal amount of water; stir into juices and cook, stirring, until thickened. Pass gravy at the table. Makes 6 to 8 servings.

A Thrifty Approach to Beef

Do some homework on meat cuts. Most of the economy cuts we buy come from the chuck (or shoulder) and the round (or leg). Both chuck and round are large sections made up of several muscles, and they vary in tenderness and texture. Cuts from the round are particularly lean and compact. But there are also big differences in tenderness and flavor.

Top round is the most tender and flavorful part. You can broil or barbecue it, with or without tenderizer; it's juiciest if cooked to the rare or medium-rare stage. About the first 3 inches of top round make up the choicest part of all; in some markets it's called London broil.

Sirloin tip (not to be confused with top sirloin) is similar to top round in tenderness and flavor. Thin cuts, often machine tenderized, are sold as breakfast steaks or tip steaks and can be broiled quickly.

Bottom round is coarser in texture and less tender than top round or sirloin tip, but has more flavor. It's good for stews and other moist-heat cooking. When it's sliced thin for stir-fry dishes, though, its reputation for toughness goes down the drain.

Eye of the round is the most compact but least tender and flavorful part. Perhaps because of its compact shape and its name, it is popular and often priced higher than other round.

Beef chuck roast (blade or arm-bone) gives a mix of more and less tender meat. To insure tenderness when you cook the whole piece, you must use slow cooking with moist heat.

The 7-bone roast (the blade bone looks like a 7) is cut from the chuck next to the rib section.

Dill-tomato Short Ribs

Gentle braising produces a rich sauce for these dill-flavored short ribs; serve with mashed potatoes and buttered crookneck squash.

  5 to 6 pounds meaty beef short ribs
  1 tablespoon salad oil
  1 large onion, sliced
  1 teaspoon salt or garlic salt
  2 teaspoons dill weed
  2 tablespoons Worcestershire
    About 6 drops liquid hot pepper seasoning
    About 2 large tomatoes, peeled
  1 tablespoon *each* cornstarch and water

Cut the short ribs apart into serving size pieces. Pour oil into a 4 to 5-quart kettle. Add meat and cook over medium heat until nicely browned on all sides. Remove meat with a slotted spoon and set aside. Add onion to pan and cook, stirring, until limp. Stir in salt, dill, Worcestershire, and hot pepper seasoning.

Dice tomatoes and add to onions. Return meat to pan, cover, and simmer slowly until the meat is fork tender, 2½ to 3 hours. Turn meat in the sauce once or twice. Skim off fat and discard. Stir cornstarch blended with water into sauce; cook, stirring, until it boils and thickens. Makes 5 or 6 servings.

Refreshing Corned Beef

The broth from corned beef can be used for soups if you take certain preliminary steps in the cooking to minimize the saltiness of the liquid. Rinse corned meat well with running water. Place meat in a deep kettle, cover generously with water, and bring to a boil. Drain off water. Repeat the process one or two more times or until the liquid has only the slightest salty taste. Then proceed according to recipe directions.

Brisket and Soup Dinner

Corned Beef Brisket
Sour Cream Spinach Soup
Dark Bread   Butter   Mustard
Dill Pickles   Radishes
Oranges in a Basket

This is a versatile menu, as both meat and soup —made from the meat broth—can be served hot or cold and are as good on the second day as the first.

For a mellow flavor to the bright green spinach soup, blend in sour cream; for more tartness, blend in yogurt. Or you can use a combination of these dairy products, tailoring the soup precisely to taste.

  4-pound piece corned beef brisket
    Water
  1 bay leaf
  3 or 4-inch-long cinnamon stick
  1 small, whole, hot red pepper
  ½ teaspoon *each* whole coriander seed,
      allspice, and mustard seed
  1 medium-size onion, sliced
  2 packages (10 oz. *each*) frozen chopped
      spinach
  2 cups sour cream (or unflavored yogurt,
      or part unflavored yogurt and part
      sour cream)

Follow directions for Refreshing Corned Beef (see above) to reduce saltiness of corned beef and broth. Then place meat in a deep kettle and add 2 quarts water. Bring liquid to a boil, reduce heat to simmer, add bay leaf, cinnamon stick, red pepper, coriander, allspice, mustard seed, and sliced onion. Cover and simmer gently for about 4 hours or until meat is very tender when pierced.

Dip out 4 cups of the cooking liquid and pour through a wire strainer; discard residue. (Taste broth; if it is still quite salty—as occasionally happens if the corned beef has been prepared in a particularly strong brine—use instead 2 cans, *each* about 14 oz., or 4 cups regular-strength chicken broth.)

Combine the 4 cups broth with the spinach in a pan and bring to a boil, breaking spinach apart as quickly as possible. Whirl spinach mixture, a portion at a time, in blender until pureed, or rub through a wire strainer or a food mill. Add the sour cream to one portion of the spinach mixture while blending.

Blend the soup and serve (reheat, if needed —do not boil) or chill. Strain remaining brisket broth and reserve to thin the chilled soup if you prefer a thinner consistency, or for use in making other soups.

Serve the brisket hot, or chilled to slice for sandwiches, with the soup. Makes 2½ quarts soup and brisket for 6 to 8 servings.

Osso Buco

The treat of the great northern Italian *osso buco* (hollow bones) is the succulent treasure of marrow in the shanks. You can use veal, beef, or lamb shanks to make osso buco. Simmer the shanks to tenderness in a light, garlicky sauce, then serve them with risotto (page 87), hot cooked zucchini, and sauteed mushooms.

    4 to 5 pounds meaty veal or beef shanks, or
        lamb shanks, cut in about 1½-inch lengths
      Salt
    2 tablespoons olive oil or salad oil
    1 large onion, chopped
    1 cup minced, lightly packed parsley
    4 cloves garlic, minced or pressed
    2 teaspoons grated lemon peel
    1 can (about 14 oz.) or 1¾ cup regular-strength
        chicken broth
    2 teaspoons *each* cornstarch and water

Sprinkle shanks lightly with salt. In a wide frying pan or a 4 to 5-quart kettle, brown shanks on all sides in olive oil over medium-high heat; do not crowd. As pieces brown, set aside to make room for more. Set all the meat aside when browned and add onions to drippings. Cook, stirring until soft but not browned.

Mix together the parsley, garlic, and lemon peel, adding half to the onions; cover and chill the balance of the parsley mixture.

Stir the onion mixture, then add the broth and return shanks and any juices to the pan. Bring to a boil, reduce heat to simmer, and cook, covered, until meat on largest sections pulls easily from the bone (takes about 1¾ hours for lamb, 2 hours for veal, and 2½ hours for beef). Stir occasionally to prevent scorching.

Carefully lift shanks from juices, transfer to a serving tray, and keep warm. Skim off and discard fat from juices. Stir half the reserved parsley mixture into pan juices and bring to a boil. Blend cornstarch and water to a smooth paste, then stir into juices and cook until slightly thickened. Pour over the shanks and sprinkle with the remaining parsley mixture. Makes 4 or 5 servings.

Osso Buco, Southern Italian-style

If you like a deep red, spicy sauce, try the southern Italian variety of osso buco.

Serve shanks with hot cooked and buttered spaghetti, hot cooked peas, and a green salad.

    1 cup hot water
    1 package (about ½ oz.) dried European
        mushrooms (optional)
    4 to 5 pounds meaty beef or veal shanks, or
        lamb shanks, cut about 1½ inches thick
      Salt
    2 tablespoons olive oil or salad oil
    1 large onion, chopped
    2 cloves garlic, minced or pressed
    1 large carrot, finely chopped
    1 can (8 oz.) tomato sauce
    1 can (6 oz.) tomato paste
    1 can (about 14 oz.) or 1¾ cups regular-
        strength chicken broth
    ¾ teaspoon ground cinnamon
    1 teaspoon basil leaves
    ¼ teaspoon ground nutmeg
    ¼ to ½ cup freshly grated Parmesan cheese

Pour hot water over mushrooms, stir to moisten, and let stand to soften.

Sprinkle shanks lightly with salt. In a wide frying pan or 4 to 5-quart kettle, brown shanks on all sides in olive oil over medium-high heat; do not crowd. As pieces are browned, set aside to make room for more. Set all the meat aside when browned and add to drippings the onion, garlic, and carrot. Cook, stirring, until the onion is soft but not browned.

Lift mushrooms from liquid and add to pan; then pour all but the last bit of the water (containing residue) into the pan, also. (If you do not use mushrooms, add the 1 cup water to pan.) Add tomato sauce, tomato paste, chicken broth, cinnamon, basil, and nutmeg. Boil, uncovered, for about 10 minutes to reduce sauce slightly. Return shanks and any juices to pan; cover and simmer gently until largest sections of meat pull easily from the bone (takes about 1¾ hours for lamb, 2 hours for veal, and 2½ hours for beef). Occasionally stir gently.

Carefully lift shanks from sauce, arrange on a platter, and keep warm. Spoon sauce over shanks. Sprinkle with Parmesan. Makes 4 or 5 servings.

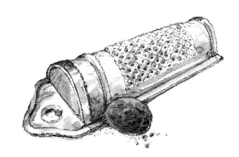

Buy Big and Freeze It

It often pays to order ground beef in 10-pound quantities or more in order to get a special price. To keep a supply in your freezer, package the meat in 1-pound portions—or even ½-pound portions if this suits your needs. Even if you use 2 or 3 pounds at a time, the smaller units thaw more quickly and give you greater flexibility in menu planning.

Country-style Cannelloni

Garlic-fragrant cheese melts inside the rolled crepes that nestle in a hearty meat sauce for this relatively quick version of cannelloni; for a more sophisticated version of this dish, such as you might find when dining in a fine Roman restaurant, see page 31.

  Meat sauce (directions follow)
  Garlic parsley (directions follow)
14 to 16 crepes (page 37)
1¼ pounds teleme or jack cheese
 1 to 1½ cups grated Parmesan cheese

A full recipe of cannelloni requires a rather large pan or shallow casserole that is suitable both for baking and serving. It may be easier for you to use several smaller containers. Choose among the following: one large, shallow container about 12 by 15 inches; two shallow containers, each at least 6 by 15 inches; or six to eight individual shallow containers, each about 3 by 6 inches.

Spread about half the meat sauce evenly over the bottom of the baking container or containers.

Divide parsley mixture equally among crepes. Cut cheese in sticks and lay an equal portion on each crepe; then roll to enclose. Place crepes seam side down, slightly apart, in meat sauce. Spoon remaining sauce over crepes to cover, then sprinkle evenly with Parmesan cheese. (At this point, you can cover and chill dish as long as 24 hours.)

Bake, uncovered, in a 450° oven for 12 to 15 minutes or until sauce is bubbling. Makes 14 to 16 cannelloni; allow 2 or 3 for a serving.

Meat sauce. Cook 1 pound lean ground beef, stirring, until it loses all pink color. Add 1 medium-size onion, finely chopped; 1 cup finely chopped, lightly packed parsley; 1 carrot, finely chopped; cook and stir until carrot is slightly soft. Open 1 can (about 1 lb.) pear-shaped tomatoes and cut through the tomatoes with a knife, dividing into smaller pieces. Pour tomatoes and juices into meat mixture. Add 1 can (about 14 oz.) or 1¾ cup regular-strength chicken broth, 1 can (6 oz.) tomato paste, and 1 teaspoon basil leaves. Boil rapidly until reduced to 4½ cups, stirring to prevent sticking. Use hot or cold; cover to chill.

Garlic parsley. Melt 1½ tablespoons butter or margarine in a frying pan over medium heat. Add 1 tablespoon minced or pressed garlic and 2 cups minced, lightly packed parsley. Cook, stirring, until parsley wilts and turns a bright green. Use hot or cold; cover if chilled.

Bobotie

The South Africans make a kind of curried meat loaf called *bobotie* (pronounced *bah-boo-tie*), laced with fruits and nuts. It is typically served with rice and chutney. Fruits such as peaches, pineapple, or bananas, sauteed in butter until lightly browned, then sprinkled with brown sugar, make appropriate accompaniments.

 ½ cup sliced almonds
 2 tablespoons butter or margarine
 2 medium-size onions, chopped
 1 tart apple, peeled and diced
 1 tablespoon curry powder
 2 pounds lean ground beef
 ½ cup fine dry bread crumbs
 2 eggs
1½ cups milk
 2 tablespoons vinegar
 2 tablespoons apricot jam or sugar
1½ teaspoons salt
 ¼ teaspoon pepper
 6 bay leaves

In a frying pan stir the nuts over medium heat in 1 tablespoon of the butter until lightly browned; set aside. Add remaining butter to pan along with onion and apple and cook, stirring occasionally, until soft (about 10 minutes). Stir in curry, cook about 1 minute, then remove from heat and let stand a few minutes or until cool enough to touch. Add to pan the ground beef, bread crumbs, 1 egg, ½ cup of the milk, vinegar, apricot jam, salt, pepper, and almonds. Use your hand to combine the ingredients well, then pack into a shallow oval or rectangular casserole (about 9 by 13 inches). Arrange bay leaves on top. Bake, uncovered, in a 350° oven for 50 minutes.

Lightly beat together the remaining 1 egg and 1 cup milk. Remove dish from oven and slowly pour mixture over the top. Return to oven for 10 minutes. Makes 7 or 8 servings.

How Much to Buy?

One pound of boned or ground meat is considered adequate for 3 or 4 adult servings. One pound of meat with relatively little bone (steaks, roasts, chops) will make 2 or 3 servings. One pound of meat with a large amount of bone (shanks—unless from high on leg, short ribs, spareribs, neck, some shoulder cuts, poultry) will usually make only 1 serving.

Allow about 3 ounces of cooked meat for a serving (boneless ready-to-eat ham, cold cuts, canned meats).

Sloppy Chinese-burgers

East meets West when you add bean sprouts, ginger, soy sauce, and Sherry to the ground beef filling of these hamburger sandwiches.

  2 tablespoons butter or margarine
  1 large onion, chopped
  1 clove garlic, minced or pressed
  2 pounds lean ground beef
  1 cup sliced celery
  1 can (4 oz.) mushroom stems and pieces
½ pound fresh bean sprouts
  1 tablespoon cornstarch
¼ teaspoon *each* pepper and ground ginger
  1 teaspoon sugar
¼ cup soy sauce
  1 tablespoon dry Sherry (optional)
    Salt
  6 to 8 hamburger buns, split and toasted
  6 or 8 green onions, thinly sliced (include some tops)
    About 2 cups shredded lettuce
    Catsup
    Soy sauce

Melt butter in a large frying pan over medium heat; add the onion and garlic and cook until onion is limp. Crumble beef into pan, add celery; cook, stirring occasionally, until meat loses its pink color. Skim off and discard fat. Drain the mushrooms, reserving the liquid, and stir mushrooms and bean sprouts into the meat mixture. Blend mushroom liquid into cornstarch, then add pepper, ginger, sugar, soy, and Sherry. Stir into meat mixture and bring to a boil; stir and cook until thickened. Season to taste with salt. Spoon meat mixture evenly over toasted bun halves and sprinkle each serving with sliced green onion. Pass lettuce, catsup, and soy sauce to add to sandwiches as desired. Makes 6 to 8 servings.

Meat Loaf in a Terrine

Terrine is the French name for the deep dish used for baking a savory ground meat mixture. It is also often used as the name for the meat loaf which is served cold, cut in slices. The meat loaf is simple to make; bake it a day ahead and chill to serve cold. It's perfect for a picnic, accompanied by cheese, green peppers, and cherry tomatoes to eat out of hand; radishes to dip into softened sweet butter; and a loaf of sourdough bread.

    About 1 pound sliced bacon
  3 or 4 chicken livers
  3 tablespoons butter or margarine
  2 small onions, chopped
1½ pounds lean ground beef (may be all or part lean ground pork)
  2 eggs
1½ teaspoons salt
¾ cup all-purpose flour, unsifted
  1 cup milk
½ to ¾ pound cooked sausages (directions follow)
  2 bay leaves
    A few whole black peppers
    French bread (optional)

Use bacon slices to line the bottom and sides of an 8 to 9-cup, deep, straight-sided casserole or loaf pan; the bacon slices should just meet in pan bottom, with ends draped over the rim.

In a frying pan, cook the chicken livers in butter for 2 or 3 minutes over moderate heat, just until firm but not fully cooked; turn once. Remove livers and add onion to pan; cook, stirring, until soft.

Beat together vigorously the ground meat, eggs, salt, and flour; blend in milk, and onions with butter.

Spoon enough meat mixture into bacon-lined casserole to make an even ½-inch-thick layer; top with chicken livers. Cover livers with a smooth layer of a little more meat. Lay the cooked sausages parallel to each other and slightly apart on meat; cover with remainder of meat; smooth top. Fold bacon over meat; lay bay leaves and peppers on bacon. Cover and bake in a 375° oven for 1 hour and 15 minutes.

Remove from heat, cool briefly, then chill thoroughly (overnight if possible). To serve, slice meat loaf vertically in casserole and lift out slices; if desired, scrape off fat. Serve meat on plate or on French bread slices. Makes 8 to 10 servings.

Cooked sausages. Use links or loops of highly seasoned sausages such as linguisa, mild Italian pork sausages, or Polish sausages. Put sausages in a saucepan, cover with water, bring to a boil, and simmer for 20 minutes. Drain well and use hot or cold.

Meatball Soup

One easygoing feature of this colorful whole-meal soup is the way you simply drop in the meatballs to poach.

Offer a whole-grain bread with the soup and then follow with a substantial dessert like the oatmeal date pie on page 90.

    2 large onions, chopped
    2 large red or green bell peppers, seeded and
          chopped
    1 cup chopped parsley
    3 tablespoons olive oil or salad oil
    ¼ cup rice
    4 cups regular-strength chicken or beef
          broth, or diluted condensed beef or
          chicken broth
    4 cups water (or use all broth)
    1 pound Swiss chard (or two 12-oz. packages
          frozen Swiss chard, thawed)
    1½ pounds lean ground beef (may be half
          lean ground lamb)
    1 egg
    ¼ cup all-purpose flour
    ½ cup milk
    1 teaspoon salt
        About 2 cups sour cream or unflavored
          yogurt

In a 5 or 6-quart kettle combine onions, peppers, parsley, and oil. Cook over medium-high heat, stirring, until vegetables are soft but not browned. Add rice, broth, and water and bring to a boil. Reduce heat to simmer.

Cut white stems from Swiss chard and chop stems; add to soup. Chop chard leaves and set aside. (If frozen chard is used, it goes into the soup after the meatballs have been added.)

Thoroughly mix together the meat, egg, flour, milk, and salt. Shape into balls about 1 inch in diameter, dropping into soup as formed. Bring soup to a boil, cover, and simmer gently 10 minutes.

Remove lid and stir in the Swiss chard leaves (or thawed frozen chard) and simmer 10 minutes more. Serve hot. If made ahead, cover to chill and then reheat to serve. Add sour cream to individual bowls, as you like. Makes about 4½ quarts (9 main-dish servings of 2-cup size).

Czech Beef Stew with Gherkins

When the Czechs make a beef stew, they're likely to be generous with paprika and mushrooms. After the meat has simmered to tenderness in a winy broth, a surprise ingredient—little pickles—gives a special tang to the stew.

    4 slices bacon
    2½ to 3 pounds boneless beef stew, cut in
          1½-inch chunks
        Salt and pepper
    ½ pound mushrooms
        About 1 tablespoon butter or margarine
    1 large onion, sliced
    1 tablespoon paprika
    ½ cup dry red wine
    1 can (14 oz.) or 2 cups regular-strength
          beef broth
    1 jar (8 oz.) sweet midget gherkin
          pickles, drained and cut in halves, lengthwise
        Hot cooked rice

Cut bacon into 1-inch lengths. In a 4 to 5-quart kettle, fry bacon until crisp; save drippings, set bacon aside.

Sprinkle beef with salt and pepper; brown in bacon drippings, stirring; set aside.

Halve or quarter mushrooms if larger than about 1 inch in diameter. Add butter to pan if needed to make a total of 2 tablespoons drippings. Add the mushrooms and onion. Cook, stirring and scraping browned bits off pan bottom, until mushrooms are limp and any juices have evaporated. Stir in paprika. Return meat and its juices to pan. Add wine and broth. Cover and simmer until meat is tender when pierced, 1½ to 2 hours. With a slotted spoon, transfer meat to a serving dish and keep warm.

Skim off and discard fat from juices. Boil juice rapidly, stirring often, until reduced to about 1 cup. Stir pickles into juices just to heat; then pour over meat and garnish with bacon. Serve over hot cooked rice. Makes 4 to 6 servings.

Stir-frying Is Thrifty

Stir-fry cooking can make a little meat seem like more. Learn from Oriental cooks how boneless meat, tender or tough, is all tender when cut in thin slices across the grain and then cooked quickly over high heat by stir-frying.

If you cook stir-fry dishes often, it pays to accumulate some small boneless pieces of beef round or chuck in your freezer. You might even decide to buy a wok (see page 23).

Meat and Vegetable Basic Stir-fry

Since you can use any lean, boneless meat and choose from a variety of vegetables to make this elementary but tasty stir-fry, you'll find this basic recipe useful to keep in mind when a quick meal is in order.

If there is any secret to this style of cooking, it's to be ready before you start—sauce mixtures blended, meat and vegetables cut—because once the pan is hot, things happen fast.

Typically served with a stir-fry would be hot cooked rice or noodles.

    1 medium-size onion
    1 pound boneless, fat-trimmed, lean beef, veal,
           pork (including ham or smoked pork),
           lamb, chicken (skin removed), or turkey
           (skin removed)
       About 4 cups cut vegetables (directions
           follow)
       Water
       Cooking sauce (directions follow)
       About 5 tablespoons salad oil
       Soy sauce

Cut onion lengthwise in eighths and separate layers. With a very sharp knife, cut meat across the grain at a slanting angle (to get wider surface) in slices about ⅛ inch thick (you can use one large piece of meat or several smaller pieces).

To cook, have onion, meat, cut vegetables, water, cooking sauce, and salad oil right by the range.

Place wok or wide frying pan over highest heat and add 1 tablespoon oil. When oil is hot enough to flow in tiny rivulets when you tilt pan, add onion and cook, stirring constantly, for about 2 minutes or until onion edges are lightly tinged with brown but onion is still crisp. Lift from pan with a slotted spoon and set aside.

Add 3 tablespoons oil to pan on high heat; when hot (as described above) add vegetables and cook,

stirring constantly, for several minutes (this varies with vegetables—quick cooking celery may take about 2 minutes, longer cooking carrots may take 5 or 6 minutes). Add water, 1 tablespoon at a time, to pan to help vegetables like carrots and broccoli cook tender without browning; always wait until all moisture is gone before adding more. When vegetables are just easy to pierce, but retain some crispness, pour from pan and set aside.

Heat another 1 tablespoon oil in pan on high heat. When hot, add half the meat and stir constantly until some pieces are lightly browned and juices have evaporated (takes 2 to 4 minutes). Add to onion. Repeat to cook remaining meat; then scoop the cooked meat back into pan and pour in cooking sauce; stir constantly until boiling, then add cooked vegetables and stir until heated through (about 1 minute). Pour into a bowl and serve; pass soy sauce. Makes 4 servings.

Cut vegetables. Choose one of the following: Cut stalky vegetables like celery, asparagus, zucchini, carrots, broccoli, in ⅛-inch-thick slices, at a slanting angle to expose more surface area on each piece. Cut mushrooms or cauliflowerets straight down through stem in ⅛-inch-wide pieces. Cut green peppers, seeded, in about 1-inch squares.

Cooking sauce. Blend 1½ cups regular-strength chicken or beef broth with 1½ tablespoons cornstarch; add 1 teaspoon sugar and 2 tablespoons *each* soy sauce and dry Sherry. Optional additions (use any or all) are 1 clove garlic, minced or pressed; ½ teaspoon grated fresh ginger root; or ¼ teaspoon ground ginger.

Storing Ginger Root

One of the most common seasonings used in wok cookery is fresh ginger root. The root can be packaged airtight and kept in your freezer; grate what you need from the frozen root without defrosting; then return it to the freezer.

Quick and Versatile: Wok Cookery

Have the thrifty ingredients used in stir-frying, and the speedy, good-tasting results you can achieve opened up a new concept in cookery for you? If so, then the wok is a utensil you should have.

The wide, deep, half-sphere shape, which evolved as a means of making maximum use of the heat from a small fire, has a number of advantages over a wide frying pan—the alternate tool for stir-frying. The high, flaring rim of the wok catches a good part of the spatter that goes with high-heat stir-frying, and the curve keeps the foods tumbling back into the hottest spot as you stir and cook. In the wok, small quantities of food are as easily cooked as larger amounts, and the small base means you can get much more cooking depth with less oil for frying than is possible in a flat pan.

Wok buying involves some decision making. How big a wok? One handle or two? Rolled steel or stainless? Accessories are numerous—you may or may not want a lid, a rack for steaming (another technique done well by the wok), a ring stand (supports the wok on a conventional range), various ladles and turners designed to fit the contours of the wok, long cooking chopsticks, wire ladles and skimmers, and cleaning brushes.

Size is a prime consideration. A wok with 14-inch top rim diameter is the size most cooks find reasonably easy to handle. A wok smaller than 12 inches in diameter is considerably less efficient; one 16 inches or larger may prove too heavy to lift comfortably (when containing food) on and off the heat as required in stir-fry cooking.

Woks have either two metal loop handles on opposite sides of the rim, or one long wooden handle. The two handle pan is less likely to tip on the heat and is easier to lift, but the handles get hot, and you will have to use potholders to hold the pan. Some cooks prefer the single handle pan because they can hold the heat resistant handle with one hand, keeping the pan quite stable, while stir-frying with the other.

The most common metal for woks is rolled steel—heavy, serviceable, and a good heat transmitter. Rolled steel does require some special care, though: it rusts if not dried carefully after use, darkens easily, and gives a slightly metallic taste to acid foods cooked in it (also typical of a heavy cast-iron frying pan—some cooks find this objectionable, others don't even notice the flavor). Woks of stainless steel are at least twice as expensive and somewhat less effective as heat conductors, but they are easier to clean and add no flavor to foods.

Rolled steel may be seasoned, if you like, though some cooks simply use the pan with no pretreatment and no difficulty. To season a wok, rub lightly with salad oil, put in a 375° oven for 30 minutes, then let cool; wash with soapy water and dry.

Scouring a wok with an abrasive material will encourage sticking; the best practice is to wash the pan with soapy water immediately after use, scrubbing away any stuck food with a stiff brush or plastic scouring pad. The brushes sold with woks for this purpose are inexpensive and many cooks find them attractive.

The lid may come with the wok; though you may use it only for steaming—to cook vegetables, keep rice hot, reheat foods—it is a useful accessory.

A rack for steaming can be simply a round cake rack; the shape of the wok holds it above the simmering water in the base of the pan.

On a gas or electric range, you need to set the wok directly on the element to get as much heat as possible for stir-frying. For frying in any quantity of oil (such as deep-frying potatoes) or for steaming, you need to cradle the wok in the adaptor ring that sits around the element. If possible, adjust so the pan is in contact with an electric element (try inverting the ring so the wide side is up) if you fry often, as there is some indication that prolonged heating of an element without contact with the cooking pan may decrease its life.

A large metal spoon and a slotted metal spoon are as useful as the special ladles, turners, and chopsticks for wok cooking, but not as decorative. The fine wire strainer ladle, though, is especially good for retrieving tiny particles from oil when frying.

Try a Slender Steak

Three poorly understood beef steaks—skirt steak, flank, and hanging tenderloin—can be tender and delicious when simply laid out flat and broiled, barbecued, or pan fried. But they must be cooked to no more than medium rare; beyond this they become rather chewy. Because the steaks are relatively thin and have fibers running the length of the cut (unlike rib and loin steaks which are cut across the grain), you get nicer sized servings, and pieces that are easier to eat, when you cut the cooked meat in slanting, thin slices across the grain.

You may have to make certain requests of your meatman when you buy these cuts:
• Don't mechanically tenderize any of them.
• Leave skirt steaks flat (typically they are rolled into pinwheels) and strip or cut off as much fat as possible. (Skirts weigh about ¾ pound each and come from inside the rib cage; there are two per beef.)
• Leave flank flat and trim any excess fat. (Two flanks, each weighing about 1½ pounds, come from each beef.)
• Trim any excess fat from hanging tenderloin. (This cut is often ground, so you may have to order ahead; it weighs about 1½ pounds and there is only one to an animal.)

All the steaks take well to robust marinades but are quite flavorful with no more seasoning than salt and pepper.

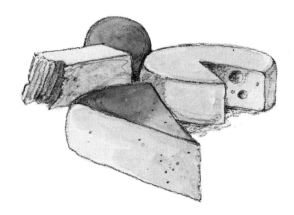

Spinach-stuffed Veal Breast

From the south of France comes an elegant stuffing for that usually inexpensive cut of veal—the breast. What it may lack in meatiness is balanced by the spinach, ground meat, mushroom, and cheese filling that is artfully seasoned with tarragon. It's company fare and worth the effort.

 2 tablespoons olive oil or salad oil
¼ pound *each* ground ham and veal or ½ pound lean ground beef
 3 slices bacon, finely chopped
½ pound mushrooms, finely chopped
 1 cup finely chopped onion
 1 large clove garlic, minced or pressed
1¼ teaspoons tarragon leaves
⅓ cup finely chopped parsley
 Cooked spinach (directions follow)
¾ cup shredded Gruyere or Swiss cheese
 1 cup soft bread crumbs
 1 egg
1½ teaspoons salt
¼ teaspoon pepper
3½ to 4-pound veal breast, split to form a pocket
 About ¼ teaspoon thyme leaves
 1 bay leaf, crushed

Heat 1 tablespoon of the oil in a large frying pan; add ground meats, bacon, and mushrooms and cook on medium heat, stirring occasionally, until mixture has browned, and juices have evaporated. Add onion, garlic, 1 teaspoon of the tarragon, and parsley to meat mixture and continue cooking until onion is soft (about 10 minutes), stirring occasionally. Remove meat mixture from heat and combine with spinach, cheese, bread crumbs, egg, salt, and pepper; mix together until thoroughly combined.

Pack stuffing lightly into veal breast cavity. Fasten edges securely with small skewers or sew with string to hold stuffing inside. Place meat, fat side up, in greased roasting pan; rub on remaining oil and sprinkle with remaining tarragon, thyme, and bay leaf.

Cover pan and bake for about 2¼ hours in 350° oven; remove cover and bake for about 15 minutes longer or until lightly browned. Remove fasteners; transfer meat to platter and slice between bones to serve. Accompany with pan juices to spoon over portions. Makes 6 to 8 servings.

Cooked spinach. Use either fresh or frozen spinach. For frozen chopped spinach, let 2 packages (10-oz. size) thaw completely, then squeeze out excess moisture.

For fresh spinach, purchase about 2 pounds. Pinch off stems, roots, and wilted or yellowed leaves. Immerse leaves in a quantity of water, swishing about to dislodge soil. Lift leaves from water and repeat washing at least 2 more times. Let drain in a colander; when no longer dripping, place leaves in a kettle. Cover and set on low heat. After 1 or 2 minutes the leaves begin to wilt; stir once, and when all the leaves are wilted but still bright green, dump back into the colander to drain. When cool, squeeze out excess moisture, then chop leaves.

Veal Caraway Stew

Veal stew is often a surprisingly good buy, comparable in price to lamb stew. Try it in this flavorful Slavic dish, pungent with caraway seed.

2½ to 3 pounds boneless veal stew, cut in 1½-inch cubes
    Salt and pepper
4 tablespoons (⅛ lb.) butter or margarine
1 large onion, chopped
2 medium-sized carrots, chopped
2 teaspoons caraway seed
1 can (about 14 oz.) or 1¾ cups regular-strength chicken broth
    Hot cooked noodles or spatzle (page 87)
    Chopped parsley

Sprinkle meat with salt and pepper. In a 4 or 5-quart kettle, melt 3 tablespoons of the butter over medium heat. Add meat and brown well. Remove meat and set aside. If needed to make about 2 tablespoons drippings, add remaining butter to pan. Add onion, carrots, and caraway seed and cook, stirring and scraping bits off pan bottom, until onion is limp. Return meat and accumulated juices to pan, then pour in chicken broth. Cover and simmer until meat is tender when pierced (about 1 hour).

With a slotted spoon, lift meat from pan and set aside. Then turn heat high and cook juices rapidly, stirring often, until reduced to about ¾ cup; return meat to pan, heating through. Serve over hot buttered noodles. Sprinkle with chopped parsley. Makes 4 to 6 servings.

Understanding Baby Beef

Next time you buy beef, you may have the option of choosing more attractively priced baby beef instead of the regular grain-fed meat; this depends, though, upon such economic factors as the cost of grain and the abundance of beef. Sold as calf, light beef, California baby beef, and mature veal, it needs to be cooked somewhat differently from the beef you're used to.

The difference comes from the size of the animal and its feed. Baby beef are 7 to 10 months old, weigh 400 to 600 pounds, and have had a diet of milk and grass. The flavor of baby beef is milder than beef but stronger than veal. The cuts are considerably smaller than beef and slightly larger than veal. The meat is light red with little marbling and a thin covering of outside fat. Though baby beef has fewer calories and less saturated fat than grain-fed beef, it has equal protein and nutritive value.

When you cook baby beef, keep these basic guidelines in mind. Because the beef is very lean, you may need to brush it frequently with melted butter, margarine, or salad oil to help brown the surface when broiling or roasting, or use these fats more generously when frying to prevent sticking. Though this young beef has little marbling, it is very tender and juicy when cooked just to rare. When well-done, it tends to become dry and chewy. If you prefer meat well-done, choose less tender cuts from shoulder or rump and braise them slowly. To preserve the mild flavor, season the baby beef lightly, as you would veal.

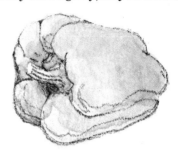

Second-start Tacos

Leftover beef—perhaps from a pot roast, a corned beef, a steak, or a roast—or even canned beef gets a flavorful new presentation.

2 tablespoons butter, margarine, or salad oil
1 medium-size onion, chopped
2 cups finely chopped or shredded cooked beef (or a 12-oz. can corned beef or chopped beef)
½ teaspoon garlic salt
1 can (4 oz.) whole California green chiles (or few drops liquid hot pepper seasoning)
1 cup shredded Cheddar or jack cheese
1 package (12) prepared taco shells
1 head iceberg lettuce, shredded
2 green onions, sliced
1 medium-size tomato, chopped

In a frying pan, heat the butter or oil and saute onion until limp. Add beef and garlic salt and heat through.

Remove seeds from chiles and discard. Chop chiles and add to meat (or add liquid hot pepper seasoning to taste). Cook, stirring, until mixture is hot and any juices have evaporated. Stir in cheese; cook, stirring, until cheese is melted; then remove from heat. Spoon equally into taco shells.

Mix together lettuce, onion, and tomato; fill taco shell with this salad. Allow 2 or 3 tacos for each serving. Serves 4 to 6.

Practical Artistry with Lamb and Pork

The shoulder of lamb and pork (including neck for stew, and front legs—shanks or ham hocks) is where the bargains reside—not because these meats have less delicious potential, but because they have more bone and take a little more effort to bring to the table than loins, hams, legs you can roast, or chops you can broil. However, extra attention to these "less tender" cuts pays off in interesting, succulent, attractive dishes (the pork pot roast with oranges on the cover is one example), many of which are highly respectable vehicles for guest meals.

Some recipes may suggest a surprise or two—a boned and rolled lamb shoulder that makes a handsome roast, lamb stew with a crunchy scattering of almonds, lamb shanks with a gleaming accent of green grapes, ground lamb in a pungent curry or a deluxe pastry overcoat. The pork dishes also run the gamut from elegant to practical: superlative cannelloni (a production worth the effort), a red chile stew, saucy ribs with a foreign spicing, and simple, nourishing soup.

A bonus is how to make crepes, the tender thin pancakes used in making cannelloni and a host of other dishes in this book.

Rolled Lamb Shoulder Roast

Though a whole shoulder of lamb is an economical cut, it becomes a noteworthy entree when it's boned, rolled, and roasted with a judicious seasoning of garlic and rosemary. Be sure to ask for the *whole* shoulder because most markets remove some of the chops first, then sell the remainder as a small, square-cut roast.

  2 cloves garlic, minced or pressed
  1 teaspoon salt
  ½ teaspoon rosemary leaves
  ¼ teaspoon pepper
    Whole lamb shoulder roast (about 6 lbs.), boned, rolled, and tied
  ½ cup water
  1½ teaspoons *each* cornstarch and water, blended smoothly

Combine garlic, salt, rosemary, and pepper. Rub mixture all over the meat and place meat on a rack in a shallow pan. Roast, uncovered, in a 350° oven for about 2 hours (or until a meat thermometer registers 145° for rare), basting occasionally with the pan juices.

Remove meat from pan and keep warm. Pour water into pan, scrape up the browned bits, and skim off and discard fat. Stir in cornstarch blended with water, bring to a boil, and cook, stirring, until thickened. Serve gravy with the roast. Makes about 8 servings.

Pilaf-stuffed Lamb Shoulder

Have your butcher cut out the knuckle and blade bone of a whole lamb shoulder, leaving the ribs and backbone. The result will be a pocket perfect for stuffing with a pilaf of golden brown rice and nuts.

    Whole lamb shoulder roast (about 6 lb.) with knuckle and blade bone removed
    Salt and pepper
  3 tablespoons butter or margarine
  ¼ cup slivered almonds or pine nuts
  1 medium-size onion, chopped
  1 cup quick-cooking brown rice
  1½ cups regular-strength chicken or beef broth
  ½ cup water
  1½ teaspoons *each* cornstarch and water, blended smoothly

Sprinkle roast with salt and pepper.

In a frying pan, melt butter over medium heat; add nuts and stir until lightly browned. Lift nuts out with a slotted spoon; set aside. Add onion and rice to pan and cook until golden; pour in the broth. Cover; simmer for 15 minutes or until liquid is absorbed. Stir in nuts.

Stuff hot rice mixture into pocket of roast. Place meat in shallow pan. Roast, uncovered, in 350° oven for about 2 hours (or until a meat thermometer registers 145° for rare); baste occasionally with pan juices.

Remove meat from pan and keep warm. Pour water into pan, scrape up the browned bits and skim off and discard fat. Stir in cornstarch blended with water, bring to a boil, and cook, stirring, until thickened. To serve, cut between the ribs; pass gravy. Makes about 8 servings.

Lamb Ragout

There's an intriguing hint of the Middle East in this simple stew—it comes from exotic touches of raisins, nutmeg, and sliced almonds. Serve the substantial lamb and rice dish with rolls, a salad made nippy by a touch of watercress, and a fruit dessert.

  3 tablespoons butter or margarine
  ⅔ cup sliced almonds
  2 tablespoons salad oil
  2½ pounds boneless lamb shoulder, cut in 1-inch cubes
  2 medium-size onions, chopped
  1 cup long grain rice
  1 teaspoon salt
  ⅛ teaspoon pepper
  ½ teaspoon ground nutmeg
  ½ cup raisins
  1 can (about 14 oz.) or 1¾ cup regular-strength chicken broth
  3 tablespoons lemon juice
    About ½ cup boiling water

Melt 1 tablespoon of the butter in a large frying pan over medium-high heat. Add almonds and cook, stirring, until golden; remove from frying pan and set aside.

(Recipe continued on next page)

Heat oil in frying pan over medium-high heat. Add lamb and cook, stirring, until brown; remove with slotted spoon. Reduce heat and melt the 2 tablespoons butter in pan. Add onions and rice and cook, stirring, until rice is opaque. Stir in salt, pepper, nutmeg, raisins, broth, and lemon juice. Return meat to pan. Reduce heat to low; cover; simmer for about 1 hour or until lamb is tender. Stir in boiling water as needed to keep rice from sticking.

Spoon the lamb and rice into serving dish and heap the almonds in the center. Makes 6 servings.

What's In a Stew?

Lamb stew is sometimes less expensive than beef stew, and it cooks tender in half the time. So keep your stew plans flexible next time you shop, comparing the prices of the two meats before deciding on your menu. You may find it less costly to try a flavorful lamb dish, such as the Caribbean stew below.

Baked Lamb Stew with Yams

Stew is a familiar family-warming dish the world over. But this spicy lamb version from the Caribbean has some real surprises, such as unripe bananas. Choose green-skinned, very firm bananas; cooked, they resemble potatoes more than fruit. Yams, baked alongside in the same oven, accompany this dish.

2½ pounds boneless lamb stew, cut in 1½-inch cubes
  2 medium-size onions, chopped
  1 or 2 cloves garlic, minced or pressed
1½ teaspoons ground coriander
  1 teaspoon oregano leaves
  ½ teaspoon ground cumin seed
  ¼ teaspoon *each* ground ginger and ground cloves
  2 tablespoons soy sauce
  1 cup water
  6 to 8 medium-size yams or sweet potatoes
  ¼ cup all-purpose flour
  1 can (about 14½ oz.) pear-shaped tomatoes
  6 medium-size carrots, cut in thick diagonal slices
  3 green-skinned bananas, peeled and cut in thick diagonal slices
    Salt and pepper

Put meat in shallow casserole (about 9 by 13 inches). Distribute onion and garlic over meat. Sprinkle with coriander, oregano, cumin, ginger, and cloves; add soy sauce and water. Cover and bake in a 425° oven for 1½ hours. At the end of 1¼ hours, put the yams into the oven around the casserole.

Blend flour smoothly with some of the tomato juice. Add this mixture, tomatoes and remaining juice, and carrots and bananas to stew when it has baked 1½ hours. Stir, cover, and continue to bake 30 minutes longer until meat, vegetables, and yams are all tender when pierced. Season to taste with salt and pepper.

Serve stew with yams, spooning juices over them. Makes 6 to 8 servings.

Lamb Shanks with Green Grapes

The elegance of this simple dish lies in the jewel-like garnish of brilliant green grapes. Lamb shanks are baked in a rich broth, which then combines with rice to make a savory pilaf. At the last moment, grapes are swirled briefly in hot butter and spooned over the lamb.

  4 lamb shanks, with bones cracked
  3 cups regular-strength chicken broth
1½ cups pearl or long grain rice
  2 tablespoons butter or margarine
  2 cups seedless green grapes

Place lamb shanks in a deep 3-quart casserole; add chicken broth. Cover and bake in a 375° oven for 2 to 2½ hours or until meat is tender when pierced. Drain broth and reserve. Cover lamb and return to oven; turn off heat.

Lightly brown rice in 1 tablespoon of the butter, stirring. Add 3 cups of broth from the lamb. Bring to a boil, cover, and reduce heat to very low. Cook 20 minutes or until rice is tender; stir occasionally. Arrange rice in a dish and top with lamb.

At once, melt 1 more tablespoon butter in frying pan over high heat. Add the grapes; stir, heating just until bright green. Spoon over lamb and rice. Makes 4 servings.

Lamb Shank Borscht

Center a family feast around this hearty, lamb-filled soup. You can tell the inspiration is Russian by the beets and cabbage that are simmered in the stock and by the garnish of dill-seasoned sour cream. Serve the borscht with a simple salad and a loaf of crusty rye bread. Finish the meal with apples and a sharp Cheddar cheese.

    6 lamb shanks, with bones whole or cracked
    1 large can (47 oz.) or 6 cups regular-
        strength chicken broth
 1½ cups water
    1 bay leaf
    6 whole black peppers
    1 teaspoon salt
    1 small green pepper, seeded and diced
    3 medium-size carrots, diced
    1 medium-size onion, finely chopped
    4 small beets, diced
    4 cups finely shredded cabbage
    1 small potato, diced
    2 tablespoons lemon juice
      Lemon wedges (optional)
      Sour cream sprinkled with dill weed
        (optional)

Put lamb shanks, chicken broth, water, bay, black pepper, and salt in a large kettle. Cover and simmer until lamb is tender, about 2 hours. (At this point you can, if you wish, cool, cover, and refrigerate the soup.) Skim or lift off fat and discard. Strain broth and discard black pepper and bay. Return shanks (or just the meat) to the stock, add green pepper, carrots, onion, beets, cabbage, and potato; bring to a boil and then simmer 15 to 20 minutes or until vegetables are tender. Remove from heat; stir in lemon juice. Ladle lamb, vegetables, and broth into bowls. Garnish each serving with a lemon wedge and dollop of dill-seasoned sour cream, if you wish. Makes 6 servings.

Keema Curry

In northern India, where this ground lamb curry originated, the cook has to grind all the spices and mince the lamb. It's easier here—our supermarkets have the supplies ready to go for this quick-to-make dish.

As you eat it, make the curry as hot as you like by adding cayenne or liquid hot pepper seasoning. The yogurt condiment serves as the cooling balance.

    2 tablespoons butter or margarine
    2 tablespoons salad oil or shortening
    2 medium-size onions, chopped
    2 cloves garlic, minced or pressed
    2 teaspoons minced fresh ginger root (or ½
        teaspoon ground ginger)
      About 2 small, dried hot red peppers,
        seeded and crushed
    2 teaspoons ground turmeric
    1 teaspoon salt
    1 medium-size tomato, peeled and diced
    2 pounds ground lean lamb
    1 package (10 oz.) frozen peas, thawed
    1 teaspoon ground coriander
  ¼ teaspoon pepper
  ⅛ teaspoon *each* ground cinnamon, ground
        cumin seed, and ground cloves
      About 1 tablespoon minced coriander or
        minced parsley
      Yogurt condiment (recipe follows)

Melt butter with salad oil in a large frying pan. Add onion, garlic, and ginger; saute until onion is lightly browned. Add red peppers, turmeric, salt, and tomato; stir and cook about 5 minutes on medium-high heat. Add lamb and cook, stirring until meat has lost its pinkness (about 10 minutes). Stir in peas, ground coriander, pepper, cinnamon, cumin seed, and cloves. Cover; simmer for 4 to 5 minutes. Stir in coriander.

Pass yogurt condiment to spoon over curry. Makes 6 to 8 servings.

Yogurt condiment. Blend 1½ tablespoons crushed dried mint leaves or ⅓ cup fresh minced mint leaves, ¼ teaspoon salt, and ⅛ teaspoon pepper with 2 cups unflavored yogurt. Cover and chill until time to serve.

Compare the Price

If you plan a ground beef dish for dinner, but lean ground lamb is a better buy, consider it as an alternative. The same seasonings are suited to both meats and are interchangeable. Your dish will have a new personality and may become a new favorite.

Spicy Lamb Chile

Ground lamb or pork gives a novel twist to the flavor of this kidney bean chile. Spoon the thick, well-seasoned mixture over pieces of hot cornbread and top with chopped raw onion and shredded Cheddar cheese. Accompany with a crisp green salad or cabbage slaw.

(Recipe continued on next page)

2 pounds lean ground lamb (or lean ground pork or lean ground beef, or any combination of these meats)
1 large onion, chopped
2 cloves garlic, minced or pressed
1 can (8 oz.) tomato sauce
1 can (6 oz.) tomato paste
1 teaspoon *each* celery salt and caraway seed
¼ to ½ teaspoon crushed hot red pepper
2 tablespoons chile powder
½ bay leaf, crumbled
1 teaspoon basil leaves
1 large can (1 lb. 11 oz.) red kidney beans
Salt and pepper

In a large kettle over medium-high heat, crumble the lamb. Cook, stirring, until meat is browned and most of the juices have evaporated; discard any excess fat. Add onion and garlic and cook, stirring, until onions are limp and translucent. Stir in tomato sauce, tomato paste, celery salt, caraway seed, red pepper, chile powder, bay leaf, and basil. Add kidney beans and liquid. Bring to a boil; then reduce heat, cover, and simmer gently for about 30 minutes to blend flavors.

If you like thick chile, continue cooking, uncovered, stirring occasionally, until mixture is reduced to the thickness you like. Season to taste with salt and pepper. Makes 8 to 10 servings.

Lamb and Mushroom Pirog

For an elegant main dish presentation on a par with elaborate beef Wellington (beef filet in pastry), consider a handsome, Russian-style *pirog*. The savory fragrance of the ground lamb and mushroom filling nestled in the golden yeast crust is most appealing.

Round out the menu with an oil-and-vinegar dressed romaine salad, and a light dessert, such as strawberries served with a generous splash of fresh orange juice.

½ cup warm water (lukewarm for compressed yeast)
1 package yeast, active dry or compressed
½ teaspoon salt
2 teaspoons sugar
3 eggs
½ cup (¼ lb.) soft butter or margarine
3½ cups all-purpose flour, unsifted
Salad oil
Lamb and mushroom filling (directions follow), chilled
1 egg yolk beaten with 1 tablespoon water

Measure water into a large bowl, stir in the yeast, and let stand about 5 minutes. Then stir in salt, sugar, and eggs. Cut butter in small pieces and add to liquid. Add the flour and mix with a heavy spoon until moistened. Shape into a compact ball with your hands and place on a floured board; knead until smooth and elastic (about 5 minutes). Rinse mixing bowl, dry it, and coat with salad oil. Place dough in bowl and turn dough over once to oil surface. Cover and let rise in a warm place until dough is about double in volume (takes at least an hour).

Knead dough on a lightly floured board to remove air bubbles. Pinch off a portion about ½-cup size and set aside; then shape the large lump of dough into a smooth ball. Lightly flour a pastry cloth (or heavy muslin towel) and roll ball of dough out on it to a rectangle 10 by 18 inches. Spoon cold lamb and mushroom filling onto half of dough toward one end. With hands, shape filling into compact rectangle, leaving about 1½-inch margin on the three outside edges. Using cloth to guide, lift exposed section of dough and lay it over filling. Neatly lap bottom edge up over the sides and pinch firmly around top rim.

Place a greased rimless baking sheet, topside down, on the pirog. Supporting with the pastry cloth and baking sheet, invert pirog onto baking sheet.

Roll reserved dough into a rectangle about 3 or 4 inches by 12 inches and cut in ½-inch-wide strips, 12 inches long. Arrange the dough strips decoratively over the top of the pirog, tucking the ends of dough beneath the pirog with fingers or tip of a knife.

Let rise in a warm place for about 20 minutes. Brush exposed surfaces with egg-water mixture. Prick top of dough in 6 to 8 places with a fork. Bake in a 350° oven for 50 minutes or until dough

is richly browned. Serve pirog hot, cut in rectangles.

To bake ahead, cool hot pirog thoroughly on a wire rack. Wrap and chill as long as 24 hours. Place cold, unwrapped pirog on an ungreased baking sheet, cover loosely with foil, and bake in a 350° oven for 50 minutes. Makes 6 to 8 servings.

Lamb and mushroom filling. Melt 3 tablespoons butter or margarine in a large frying pan. Add 2 pounds thinly sliced mushrooms, mix with butter, cover, and cook over medium heat for about 5 minutes to draw out juices; stir occasionally.

Remove cover, turn heat high, and cook, stirring frequently, for about 10 minutes or until all the liquid has boiled away. Mix in 2 tablespoons all-purpose flour, 2 teaspoons dill weed, and ½ cup sour cream; cook, stirring, until bubbling and blended. Pour mushroom mixture into a large bowl and set aside. Rinse frying pan and add to it 1½ pounds lean ground lamb. Cook over high heat, stirring in and breaking up meat until it is richly browned. Skim off and discard fat. Stir lamb into mushroom mixture and add ¾ teaspoon salt (or to taste). Cover and chill thoroughly.

You Can Be Sure It's Tender

Lamb chops come in all shapes, sizes, and prices, but one tip to remember is that all chops, whether from shoulder, loin, or leg, are tender enough for dry-heat cooking—broiling, barbecuing or pan frying.

Cannelloni Roma

This elegant dish is an example of how effort instead of expensive ingredients can produce a truly impressive entree. There are several steps in making the filling, sauces, and crepes, and each can be completed at a convenient time; the cannelloni can be assembled and ready to bake the day before your party.

Cannelloni go well with a crisp green salad and a vegetable such as artichokes or zucchini, complemented by a mellow red wine. For dessert, pour white wine and sugar over peaches or pears, or serve frozen slabs of spumoni.

Meat filling (directions follow)
14 to 16 crepes (page 37)
Tomato sauce (directions follow)
Bechamel sauce (directions follow)
About 4 cups shredded fontina or jack
    cheese

Divide meat filling into ¼-cup-size portions (or equally among crepes) and spoon a portion of filling down the center of each crepe. Roll to enclose filling.

Blend tomato sauce with bechamel sauce and spoon all the blended sauce equally into the baking containers (you will need one large shallow container about 12 by 15 inches; two shallow containers, each at least 6 by 15 inches; or 6 to 8 individual shallow containers, each about 3 by 6 inches).

Set filled crepes, seam side down, side by side and slightly apart in sauce coated pans. Sprinkle evenly with cheese to cover entire surface of crepes. At this point you can cover and chill as long as 24 hours.

Bake uncovered in a 450° oven for 12 to 15 minutes, or until sauce is bubbling and filling is hot. Serve at once. Makes 14 to 16 cannelloni; allow 2 or 3 for a main-dish serving or 1 for a first-course serving.

Meat filling. In a frying pan, cook 1 large onion, chopped, in 2 tablespoons butter, margarine, salad oil, or olive oil until soft. Add to pan 1 pound boneless pork shoulder or butt or loin end, cut in ½-inch cubes. Cover and cook over medium to medium-low heat, stirring often, for 15 minutes (juices simmer as they accumulate). Add ¼ teaspoon ground nutmeg, ½ cup chopped, lightly packed parsley, and 3 large chicken thighs (about ¾ lb. total weight), boned, skinned, and cut in ½-inch cubes.

Cover and continue to simmer another 15 minutes. (If the mixture begins to brown, add water, 1 tablespoon at a time to keep slightly moist.) Let cool.

Force meat mixture (including any juices) and ⅛ pound cooked ham or prosciutto (Italian-style ham—optional) through medium blade of a food chopper. Mix well with 2 whole eggs, ½ cup grated Parmesan cheese, 1 cup ricotta cheese, and salt to taste. Cover; chill until ready to use.

Tomato sauce. Cook 1 medium-size onion, finely chopped, in 2 tablespoons butter, margarine, salad oil, or olive oil until soft. Add 1 cup finely chopped, lightly packed parsley; 1 carrot, finely chopped; and 1 red bell pepper, seeded and finely chopped (or 2 canned whole pimentos, finely chopped); cook, stirring, until carrot is slightly soft.

Drain liquid from 1 can (about 1 lb.) pear-shaped tomatoes into vegetables; chop tomatoes. Add tomatoes and juices, 1 can (about 14 oz.) or 1¾ cup regular-strength chicken broth, and 1 teaspoon basil leaves to vegetables. Boil rapidly, stirring frequently, until reduced to 2 cups (most of the liquid is evaporated). Add salt to taste. Use hot or cold; cover if chilled.

(Recipe continued on next page)

Bechamel sauce. Mince 1 medium-size onion and cook until soft in 4 tablespoons (⅛ lb.) butter or margarine. Blend in 3 tablespoons all-purpose flour, remove from heat, and gradually add ¾ cup regular-strength chicken broth, 1 cup milk, and ¼ teaspoon ground nutmeg. Simmer, uncovered, stirring frequently, until reduced to 1½ cups; takes about 15 minutes. Salt to taste. Use hot or cold; cover to chill.

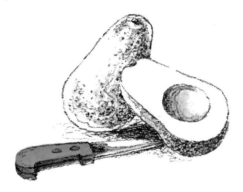

Baekeoffe

To make this classic Alsatian pork and veal dish, just put everything together in one casserole and let it bubble away in the oven until the meat is tender. Then lift the lid, and you'll find a wine-fragrant stew. Serve it in wide soup bowls; pass chunks of crusty bread and accompany with a basket of assorted crisp vegetables: cauliflower, green onions, radishes, carrots, mushrooms.

  4 medium-size new potatoes (about 1½ lb.), peeled and cut in ¼-inch slices
  1 pound boneless pork shoulder or butt, cut in 1-inch cubes
  1 pound boneless veal stew, cut in 1-inch cubes
  2 medium-size onions, thinly sliced
 ⅓ cup finely chopped parsley
  2 cloves garlic, minced or pressed
  2 bay leaves
1½ teaspoons salt
 ¼ teaspoon pepper
1¾ cups dry white wine (a Rhine wine such as Riesling, Gewurztraminer, or Sylvaner)
 ¼ cup (⅛ lb.) butter or margarine

Lightly grease a 3 or 4-quart shallow casserole; layer in half the potatoes; top with half the pork and half the veal; then add half the onions and half the parsley, 1 clove garlic and 1 bay leaf. Repeat with remaining potatoes, pork, veal, onions, parsley, and garlic, finishing with a bay leaf. Sprinkle salt and pepper over all; pour in wine and dot pieces of butter on top.

Cover and bake in a 375° oven for about 1 hour and 30 minutes or until meats are tender. Ladle with juices into soup bowls. Makes 6 to 8 servings.

Carnitas

A Mexican picnic inspired this colorful, easygoing meal—soft, warm corn tortillas enfold succulent bits of simmered then baked pork, and guacamole, refried beans, and lettuce. Accompany with green onions, radishes, and cherry tomatoes. Have sliced oranges or pineapple for dessert and sangria or beer for the beverage.

4½ to 5-pound pork shoulder or butt (do not have bone cut)
    Water
1½ teaspoons salt
 ½ teaspoon *each* oregano leaves, ground cumin seed, whole or crushed coriander seed
  2 medium-size onions, chopped
  2 carrots, chopped
    About 3 cups shredded iceberg lettuce
    Mild pickled chiles
    Guacamole (recipe follows)
  2 cans (1 lb. *each*) refried beans, heated
    Hot corn tortillas (directions follow)

Place pork shoulder in a deep, close-fitting pan and just barely cover with water. Add salt, oregano, cumin, coriander, onions, and carrots. Bring water to a boil, cover pan, and simmer meat gently for 2½ hours. Lift meat from broth and place in a baking pan (save broth for soups). Bake, uncovered, in a 350° oven for 45 minutes to 1 hour or until meat is very well browned. Drain off all fat. Place meat in serving dish; surround with lettuce and mild pickled chiles. Cut meat in chunks or pull apart and serve; accompany with guacamole, refried beans, and hot corn tortillas. Make into tacos by putting all the ingredients in a tortilla, or simply eat from a plate with knife and fork, eating the tortillas as bread. Makes 8 to 10 servings.

Guacamole. Peel and seed 2 large ripe avocados and mash coarsely with a fork. Blend in 3 tablespoons lime or lemon juice, 4 canned California green chiles (seeded and chopped), ¾ teaspoon ground coriander or 2 teaspoons minced coriander and about ½ teaspoon salt, or to taste. Garnish with tomato wedges and parsley.

Hot corn tortillas. Allow 3 or 4 corn tortillas for each serving. Moisten your hands in water and rub them over the surface of a tortilla. Place the dampened tortilla in an ungreased frying pan (or on a griddle) over medium-high heat and turn every few seconds, using your fingers or a spatula to flip it, until the tortilla is very hot and pliable. Put immediately into a tightly covered dish, or put into a foil packet, seal it, and hold in a warm oven (about 200°) until all tortillas are heated. (The secret is to keep them moist once hot.)

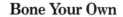

Bone Your Own

Bone your own pork for recipes in this chapter that call for the boneless meat. The cuts specified have large, easy-to-find bones, and you'll find it takes only a few minutes to cut them out with a sharp, short-bladed knife. Just follow along with the blade close to the bone.

A Pot Roast Dinner

Green Salad
Pork Pot Roast with Oranges
Pot Roasted Onions and New Potatoes
Italian Green Beans
French Bread   Butter
Crepes (page 37) with Jam and Whipped Cream

While the pork is braising to tenderness in the oven or on top of the range, you have time to wash and crisp the greens for the salad and to make the crepes. (You'll have even more time if you keep a supply of crepes in your freezer.) Serve fresh (or frozen) Italian green beans, if available; otherwise serve regular green beans, allowing 1½ to 2 pounds for 6 to 8 servings.

The dessert is really more a matter of assembling than it is a recipe. Seal in foil 12 to 16 (enough for 6 to 8 servings) crepes (thawed if frozen) and place in a 325° oven for about 10 minutes to heat through. Fold each crepe in half, then in half again to make a triangle, and arrange on a platter or individual plates. Pass a berry jam and a bowl of sweetened whipped cream (use 1 cup whipping cream) to spoon on each serving.

Pork pot roast with oranges. Small onions and new potatoes share the kettle with the roast.

- 4 to 4½-pound boned, rolled, and tied pork shoulder loin or loin end roast
- 1 large onion, finely chopped
- 2 teaspoons mustard seed
- ½ teaspoon ground cinnamon
- ¼ teaspoon ground nutmeg
- 2 teaspoons grated orange peel
- 1 can (about 14 oz.) or 1¾ cup regular-strength chicken broth
  Water
- 12 to 16 red-skinned new potatoes (*each* about 1½ inches in diameter)
- 12 to 16 boiling onions (*each* about 1 inch in diameter)
- 2 teaspoons *each* cornstarch and water
- 2 medium-size oranges
  Chopped parsley and parsley sprigs

In a 4 to 5-quart kettle, brown pork well in its own fat over medium-high heat, turning frequently. When browned, add chopped onion, mustard seed, cinnamon, and nutmeg and stir until onion is soft. Add 1 teaspoon of the orange peel and the broth; stir well to loosen any browned particles. Cover pan tightly. Simmer on top of the range for about 2 hours or until meat is tender when pierced. (Or transfer, if you like, to 4 to 5-quart casserole you can serve from, and bake in a 375° oven for about 2 hours.) Check occasionally, and if the liquid level is less than about ½ inch deep, add water to bring up to this level.

If desired, peel a center band from each potato (for decoration). Tuck the potatoes and onions in around meat, into the juices as much as possible. Let cook about 30 to 40 minutes or until vegetables are tender when pierced; check liquid level occasionally.

Meanwhile peel oranges with a knife, cutting off all white membrane; cut in crosswise slices and set aside.

Transfer vegetables and meat (support with 2 large spoons as it is quite tender) from pan to a rimmed platter, and keep warm. (If the meat bakes in a serving casserole, drain juices into a small pan.) If necessary, boil juices until reduced to about 1 cup (or add water if needed); skim off and discard fat. Blend cornstarch smoothly with water and stir into boiling juices; cook until thickened.

Drizzle juices over meat and vegetables, tuck orange slices in among the vegetables, and sprinkle with remaining orange peel. Garnish with chopped parsley and parsley sprigs.

Slice meat in about ½-inch-thick pieces and serve with vegetables, fruit, and sauce. Makes 8 to 10 servings.

Pork and Sauerkraut Stew

Sauerkraut and dill weed give a lively zip to this pork stew; a touch of sour cream adds smoothness. You can rinse the sauerkraut before adding it to the pork, if you want a milder taste.

1 large can (about 22 oz.) sauerkraut
2½ to 3 pounds boneless lean pork shoulder or butt, cut into 1½-inch cubes
   Salt and pepper
3 tablespoons butter or margarine
1 large onion, chopped
2 cloves garlic, minced or pressed
2 teaspoons paprika
1½ teaspoons dill weed
1 can (about 14 oz.) or 1¾ cups regular-strength chicken broth
½ cup sour cream blended with 2 teaspoons cornstarch
   Chopped parsley

Drain sauerkraut; rinse, if desired, for milder flavor, then drain again. Sprinkle pork cubes with salt and pepper.

Melt 2 tablespoons butter in a 4 to 5-quart kettle over medium heat. Add meat and brown well, stirring. Lift out meat; set aside. Add the 1 tablespoon butter, if needed, to make about 2 tablespoons fat in the pan. Add onion and garlic and cook, stirring and scraping bits off pan bottom, until onion is limp. Stir in paprika and dill weed. Return meat and accumulated juices to pan. Add chicken broth and the drained sauerkraut. Cover and simmer until meat is tender (about 1 hour and 15 minutes).

Skim off and discard fat. Increase heat and cook rapidly, uncovered, stirring often, until sauce is reduced to about ¾ cup. Add sour cream and stir until simmering. Spoon into a serving dish and sprinkle with parsley. Makes 6 to 8 servings.

The Byword Is Flexibility

Be prepared to shift gears; if you're shopping for pork shoulder for stew, and loin end is a better price—then buy loin end.

Braised Pork with Red Chile Sauce

Spicy red chile sauce, tempered by a touch of whipping cream, complements cubes of tender, mild pork. Serve the dish over rice, with a green garnish of avocado and green onions.

3 pounds lean pork shoulder or butt, boned
2 tablespoons salad oil
2 large onions, chopped
2 cloves garlic, minced or pressed
5 to 6 teaspoons chile powder
1 teaspoon ground cumin
1½ teaspoons oregano leaves
1¼ cups water
1½ teaspoons salt
3 tablespoons canned tomato paste
½ cup whipping cream
1 avocado, peeled and sliced
⅓ cup thinly sliced green onions (tops included)
   Hot cooked rice
2 limes or lemons, cut in wedges

Trim excess fat from meat and cut into 1-inch cubes. In a large frying pan, heat the oil over medium-high heat; add meat and lightly brown, stirring. Push to sides of pan, add onion, garlic, chile powder, cumin, and oregano; saute until onion is limp. Stir in water, salt, and tomato paste; simmer, covered, until pork is tender when pierced (about 1 hour). Skim off fat and discard. Stir in cream and cook, stirring, until sauce boils.

Spoon into a serving dish and garnish with avocado and green onions. Serve with rice and offer lime to squeeze over. Makes 7 or 8 servings.

Braised Pork with Green Chile Sauce

The green color of this unusual stew comes from California green chiles, green peppers, and coriander. Serve spooned into warm flour tortillas, adding sour cream, fresh tomato, and a squeeze of lime. Or ladle the stew over rice. Either way, it goes well with a green salad and, for dessert, a fresh melon.

3 pounds lean pork shoulder or butt, boned
2 tablespoons salad oil
1 large onion, chopped
2 cloves garlic, minced or pressed
2 large green peppers, seeded and chopped
1 large can (about 7 oz.) California green chiles, seeded and chopped
1 teaspoon oregano leaves
½ teaspoon ground cumin
1½ teaspoons salt
½ cup chopped coriander (or 2 tablespoons dried coriander leaves)
1 tablespoon wine vinegar
¼ cup water
1 large or 2 medium-size tomatoes, cut in wedges
   About 1 cup sour cream
2 limes or lemons, cut in wedges
   Warm flour tortillas (directions follow) or hot cooked rice

Trim excess fat from meat and cut in about ¾-inch cubes. In a large frying pan, add salad oil and place over medium-high heat. Add meat to pan and lightly brown, stirring. Push meat to sides of pan and add onion, garlic, green peppers; cook until vegetables are limp. Stir in green chiles, oregano, cumin, salt, coriander, vinegar, and water; cover and simmer until meat is tender when pierced (about 1 hour). Skim off fat and discard. Cook, uncovered, until most of the sauce is evaporated, stirring occasionally.

Spoon into serving dish and garnish with tomato wedges, or have tomatoes, sour cream, and limes in separate containers. You can ladle the stew into the tortillas, adding tomatoes and sour cream and squeezing in lime; then roll to enclose filling and eat out of hand. Or spoon stew onto rice, top with sour cream, and squeeze on lime. Makes 6 to 8 servings.

Warm flour tortillas. Allow 2 to 3 flour tortillas per serving (about 7-inch size). Stack and wrap in foil. Place in a 350° oven about 20 minutes, until heated.

Swedish-style Pork Ribs

Country-style spareribs (butterflied loin end or shoulder roast) switch nationalities easily with a few simple changes in seasoning. The Swedes prepare them in a creamy, dill-flavored sauce with potatoes.

They are equally delicious in the Hungarian variation that follows. Here, the pork is seasoned with paprika and caraway and served over hot cooked noodles or spatzle (recipe on page 87).

½ teaspoon *each* salt and dill weed
¼ teaspoon thyme leaves
⅛ teaspoon pepper
3½ to 4½ pounds country-style spareribs
2 medium-size onions, chopped
⅔ cup regular-strength chicken broth or water
2 teaspoons cornstarch blended with 1 tablespoon water
½ cup sour cream
8 to 12 hot, boiled small new potatoes
   Dill weed

Rub the salt, ½ teaspoon dill weed, thyme, and pepper onto meat. Place onions in a deep 3 to 4-quart casserole; top with meat. Add broth and cover. Bake in a 425° oven for 2 hours or until meat is tender when pierced. (To make ahead, cover dish now and chill; reheat, covered, in a 375° oven for 45 minutes.)

Lift meat from casserole to a serving dish and keep warm. Skim off and discard fat from juices, then mix in cornstarch-water paste. Stir in sour cream and bring to a boil, stirring. Pour sauce over meat, ring with potatoes, sprinkle with dill weed. Makes 5 or 6 servings.

Hungarian-style Pork Ribs. Follow the preceding recipe for Swedish-style pork ribs, making these changes: Omit the dill weed and thyme; instead use 2 teaspoons paprika, 1 teaspoon dry mustard, and ¼ teaspoon caraway seed. Increase the broth or water from ⅔ cup to 1 cup and add 1 tablespoon lemon juice. Thicken the juices with 1 tablespoon cornstarch instead of 2 teaspoons, blending in ½ to ¾ cup sour cream. Serve with hot cooked noodles or spatzle (recipe on page 87). Makes 5 or 6 servings.

An Energy Saving Note

Whenever possible, it's a good idea to use your oven to cook more than one dish at a time, such as the potatoes and oven-roasted spareribs (see below). Perhaps there is room for a pie, cake, or baked fruit, too. You save not only effort, but energy—the kind you buy from the utility companies.

Oven-roasted Country-style Spareribs and Potatoes

As these spareribs bake in the oven, they form a spicy-sweet glaze. Bake the potatoes in the same oven. Accompany with cabbage salad.

(Recipe continued on next page)

4 pounds country-style spareribs
½ cup hot water
3 tablespoons soy sauce
¼ cup orange marmalade
1 clove garlic, minced or pressed
¼ teaspoon ground ginger
3 medium-size baking potatoes, scrubbed
1 tablespoon butter or margarine

Arrange spareribs, meaty side down, in a single layer in a roasting pan. Stir together the water, soy sauce, marmalade, garlic, and ginger. Pour mixture over spareribs. Bake, uncovered, in a 350° oven, basting frequently, for 1 hour (they take a total of 2 hours and 15 minutes).

When spareribs have baked for 30 minutes, put potatoes in the oven; bake for 1½ hours or until they give easily to pressure.

At the end of 1 hour, turn spareribs bone side down and continue baking, basting frequently, for about 1 hour and 15 minutes. Transfer spareribs to a serving platter and keep warm. Skim off and discard fat from pan juices; pour juices into a small serving bowl.

Melt butter in the roasting pan over medium heat on top of the range. Cut potatoes in half lengthwise. Place potatoes, cut side down, in the roasting pan and cook until cut surfaces are golden brown (about 5 minutes). Arrange potatoes on the serving platter around meat. Makes 5 or 6 servings.

Be a Bone Saver

You can add to the flavor of chicken broth (page 51) by using bones and scraps from other meats to make up the total amount of broth-making bones.

Save bones, scraps of meat, drippings, and fat from such cooked meats as hams, legs of lamb, pork or beef roasts—anything that doesn't get gnawed. Also save all the bones and scraps when you bone uncooked meat or have it boned. Store these remnants in the freezer until you accumulate a working quantity.

Indian-style Split Pea Soup

On a brisk evening, serve a warming pot of thick, spicy split pea soup, unusually seasoned with lots of curry flavoring—composed of cumin, turmeric, and coriander. A cooling cucumber salad is a nice palate refresher with the soup.

1 ham hock (about 1 lb.) cracked
  Water
1 package (12 oz.) or 1¾ cups green or yellow split peas
1 small onion, chopped
1 teaspoon *each* ground coriander and ground cumin seed
¼ teaspoon ground turmeric
1 teaspoon lemon juice
4 teaspoons sugar
  Salt and pepper
2 tablespoons chopped coriander or parsley
  About ¼ cup chopped salted peanuts

Place ham hock in a 4 to 5-quart kettle, cover with water, cover pan, and bring to a boil. Simmer 10 minutes; drain.

Sort through peas to remove any extraneous materials. Rinse peas, drain, and add to the ham hock with onion and 6 cups water. Cover and simmer for about 1½ hours or until peas mash readily. Remove ham hock, discard bone and fat, cut meat into small pieces, and return to soup. Add the ground coriander, cumin, turmeric, lemon juice, sugar, and salt and pepper to taste. Simmer 10 minutes longer. Pass fresh coriander and chopped peanuts to add to individual bowls. Makes 3 or 4 servings.

Ham Aspic

When the weather is hot, a cool meat salad makes a refreshing entree for family or guests. In this colorful adaptation of the classic French *Jambon en persil*, thin slices of cooked ham, sprigs of parsley, and green onions are suspended in a shimmering aspic.

2 envelopes unflavored gelatin
½ cup cold water
2 cans (about 14 oz. *each*) or 3½ cups regular-strength chicken broth
2 chicken bouillon cubes (or 2 teaspoons chicken stock concentrate)
2 tablespoons white wine vinegar
¼ teaspoon liquid hot pepper seasoning
½ cup *each* thinly sliced green onions and minced, lightly packed parsley
¾ pound thinly sliced cooked ham
  Mustard sauce (recipe follows)

Mix gelatin with cold water and let stand a few minutes to soften. Bring to a boil over high heat the chicken broth, bouillon cubes, vinegar, and liquid hot pepper seasoning. Add the softened gelatin, stirring until completely dissolved; remove from heat. Chill gelatin mixture until slightly thickened. Gently stir in green onions and parsley; pour mixture into a 6-cup ring mold. Using a spoon, lightly push individual slices of ham down into gelatin to create a rippled effect. Cover and chill mold until set, at least 4 hours.

To unmold, dip container up to edge of rim in hot water until edges just begin to liquefy. Cover container with serving plate and invert, turning salad out onto plate; chill to firm the surface. Cut salad in thick slices with a sharp knife and spoon mustard sauce onto slices. Makes about 6 servings.

Mustard sauce. Thoroughly mix together 1 cup mayonnaise, ½ cup sour cream, 3 tablespoons prepared mustard, and 2 teaspoons sugar.

Braendende Kaerlighed

In Denmark, this popular dish is called "Burning Love." Slowly cooked onions (they take almost 2 hours) are cradled in a mound of mashed potatoes, surrounded by crunchy bacon and pungent pickled beets. Serve burning love with dark bread and a green vegetable or salad. The Whole Wheat Carrot Cake on page 93 makes a hearty dessert.

¼ cup *each* butter or margarine and salad oil
8 large onions, thinly sliced
1 pound bacon
3 to 4 cups hot, well-seasoned mashed potatoes
1 can (1 lb.) sliced pickled beets, well drained
   Parsley sprigs

Melt butter with oil in a 12 to 14-inch frying pan over low heat; add onions and cook slowly, turning often, until they are brown and crisp (takes 1½ to 2 hours). Drain off fat and sprinkle onions with salt; put in a dish and keep warm.

In the same pan fry bacon until crisp; drain and keep warm.

To serve, arrange mashed potatoes in a mound on a platter, making a deep well in the center. Fill the well with fried onions. Surround potatoes with bacon; garnish with beets and parsley. Makes 6 servings.

Elegance Is in the Wrapper: Crepes

You can transform almost anything into an elegant dish by wrapping it in paper-thin pancakes; the French call them *crepes*. Use to make dishes like the country-style cannelloni on page 19, the Roman-style cannelloni on page 31, or the spinach and onion crepes on page 68. Or improvise with a filling of your choice—it's an excellent way to convert leftovers into show stoppers.

Also keep in mind that crepes are delicious served hot with butter and jam for breakfast or dessert.

Crepes can be made ahead, then refrigerated or frozen (either filled or unfilled) for later use.

3 eggs
⅔ cup all-purpose flour, unsifted
1 cup milk
   About 4 teaspoons butter or margarine

In a large bowl, combine eggs and flour and beat until smooth. Stir in milk.

Place a 6 to 7-inch crepe pan (or other flat-bottomed frying pan of this size) on medium heat. When pan is hot, add ¼ teaspoon butter and swirl to coat surface. At once pour in about 1½ tablespoons of the batter, tilting pan so batter flows quickly over the entire flat surface. If the heat is correct and the pan hot enough, the crepe sets at once, forming tiny bubbles (don't worry if there are a few little holes); if the pan is too cool, the batter makes a smooth layer. Cook crepe until the edge is lightly browned and the surface looks dry.

Because this crepe tears easily, use this technique for turning: Run a wide spatula around the edge to loosen (without tearing crepe). Hold spatula on top of crepe and invert with pan, turning the crepe out into the spatula. Then quickly guide the crepe, uncooked surface down, back into pan and brown lightly. Turn crepe out of pan onto plate.

Repeat this procedure to make each crepe; stir batter occasionally and stack crepes one atop another. If you don't use them within a few hours, package airtight when cool; refrigerate as long as a week or freeze for longer storage. Allow crepes to reach room temperature before separating; they tear if cold. Makes 14 to 16 crepes.

Low-cost Discoveries with Accessory Meats

With the exception of sweetbreads (notably absent here), innards or organ meats of the animals that provide roasts, steaks, chops, and stews have a hard time making it on the popularity rating sheet in American kitchens. For this reason you will note a predominance of ethnic influence in the attractively economical preparations selected for you: liver as served in Venice, tongue simmered a la Provencal, tripe in the Florentine fashion, kidneys with the German sweet-sour touch, and heart as grilled in Peru.

Additionally, there are some sausage main dishes. Sausages, technically, are perhaps not the best buy per pound, but when you consider the brief effort required to turn these seasoned packets into interesting entrees, another aspect of economy—time—justifies their use here.

Liver Stroganoff

The piquant sour cream and mushroom sauce that distinguishes beef stroganoff also complements liver. Serve with pan-fried potatoes, hot boiled noodles, white or brown rice, or a bulgur wheat pilaf.

1 pound calves liver, baby beef liver, beef liver, or lamb liver, cut in ½-inch-thick slices
  Salt and pepper
4 tablespoons all-purpose flour
4 tablespoons butter or margarine
1 large onion, finely chopped
½ pound mushrooms, thinly sliced
2 tablespoons tomato-based chile sauce
¾ cup regular-strength chicken or beef broth
2 tablespoons Sherry (optional)
½ cup sour cream
2 tablespoons chopped parsley

Remove membrane and any tubes from liver; cut liver into ½-inch-wide strips. Sprinkle lightly with salt and pepper; dredge in flour, shaking off excess and reserving flour. Melt 3 tablespoons of the butter in a frying pan over medium-high heat; add liver and cook until browned on all sides but still slightly pink inside (about 5 minutes); set liver aside.

Add remaining 1 tablespoon butter, onion, and mushrooms to pan; cook until vegetables are limp. Add remaining flour (about 1 tablespoon) and cook, stirring, 1 minute. Add chile sauce, broth, and Sherry. Cook, stirring, until thickened. Stir in sour cream, liver, and salt and pepper to taste; heat through. Sprinkle with parsley. Makes 4 servings.

Poached Liver

A chunk of liver poached in a seasoned stock develops a firm texture and succulence that clearly distinguishes it from liver that is fried or broiled.

Serve it hot, sliced wafer-thin. Or chill to serve thinly sliced like other cold cuts. You might offer the liver with a variety of accompaniments for making sandwiches: red or white mild onion rings, alfalfa sprouts or watercress, tomato or avocado slices, red or green pepper rings, pickle chips, mustard, and sour cream or cottage cheese.

2 to 2½ pounds unsliced calves liver, baby beef liver, beef liver, or lamb liver
6 whole black peppers
  About 10 sprigs parsley
1 large onion, cut in wedges
1 large carrot, cut in chunks
1 bay leaf
½ teaspoon salt
  Water

Remove membrane and any tubes from liver. Place liver, pepper, parsley, onion, carrot, bay leaf, and salt in a close-fitting pan (about 3-qt. size). Add enough water (1½ to 2 cups) to barely cover meat. Bring to a boil, cover, reduce heat, and simmer for about 45 minutes or until meat is no longer pink in center (cut a small gash to test). Serve hot; or cool in liquid, cover, and refrigerate until needed (as long as 1 week). If meat is not completely covered with liquid, turn it over daily to keep the whole piece moist. Makes 8 to 10 servings.

Sauteed Liver with Tomato Sauce

Tomatoes and mushrooms simmer together with seasonings to make a mellow topping for sauteed liver slices. The sauce can be made ahead; the liver is prepared at the last moment.

3 tablespoons butter or margarine
1 medium-size onion, sliced
1 clove garlic, minced or pressed
½ small green pepper, seeded and chopped
½ pound mushrooms, chopped
1 large can (1 lb. 12 oz.) pear-shaped tomatoes
1 small jar (2 oz.) canned pimento, chopped
¼ teaspoon salt
⅛ teaspoon pepper
1½ pounds calves liver, baby beef liver, beef liver, or lamb liver, sliced ½ inch thick
  All-purpose flour
3 tablespoons salad oil

In a pan melt butter over medium heat. Add onion, garlic, and green pepper; cook for about 5 minutes. Stir in mushrooms, tomatoes (break them up with a fork), pimento, salt, and pepper. Boil gently, uncovered, until thickened to a nice spooning consistency, or for about 15 minutes. (If made ahead, return to simmer to serve.)

Remove membrane and any tubes from slices; dredge liver in flour, shaking off excess. Heat oil in a frying pan over medium-high heat; add liver and cook until browned on both sides (still faintly pink inside—cut to test); takes about 5 minutes. Spoon sauce over liver. Makes about 6 servings.

Venetian Liver with Onions

Lemon peel is the surprising, but typically Venetian, flavor accent with liver and onions. Create a whole meal, Venice-style, by starting with a soup of hot chicken broth with green peas; then serve the liver and a salad of fresh tomato and radish slices with oil and vinegar dressing. For dessert, you might have a plate of ripe pears.

      4   large onions
    ½   cup olive oil or salad oil
    ½   teaspoon grated lemon peel
      2   pounds calves liver, baby beef liver, beef liver, or lamb liver cut in ½-inch-thick slices and trimmed of tough membrane and tubes
          All-purpose flour
          Salt and pepper

Quarter the onions and separate into layers. Place onions in a wide frying pan with oil and cook, stirring, over medium-high heat for about 10 minutes or until onions are soft and slightly golden. Stir in lemon peel; then lift onions from pan and oil with a slotted spoon and place in a bowl (this can be done several hours ahead; hold at room temperature).

Coat liver slices with flour and shake off excess; lay pieces side by side on waxed paper or a pan; sprinkle with salt and pepper.

Return frying pan with oil (in which onions were cooked) to medium heat; fill with liver slices but do not crowd. Brown liver well on both sides and cook until there is just a hint of pink color remaining in the center (cut a gash to test; takes

about 5 minutes). Transfer liver as cooked to a warm platter and keep warm; return onions to pan when liver is cooked; stir to heat through and then pour over liver. Makes 6 to 8 servings.

Beef Heart en Brochette

In Peru, this is a popular way to serve beef heart. The robust marinade suits the meat well, emphasizing its beef character.

      2   pounds beef heart, cut in ¾-inch-thick slices
      1   teaspoon *each* salt and ground cumin seed
      2   cloves garlic, minced or pressed
    ½   cup vinegar
    ¼   cup *each* water and salad oil
          Liquid hot pepper seasoning
      6   thin slices bacon
          Tomato-based chile sauce

Trim any fat and tubes from heart; rinse and drain well. Then cut slices into pieces about 1½ inches square. Combine heart with salt, cumin, garlic, vinegar, water, oil, and about ¼ teaspoon hot pepper seasoning. Cover and refrigerate 4 to 8 hours, stirring 3 or 4 times. Drain the heart, saving the marinade.

On each of 6 skewers, string about 5 heart pieces lengthwise, weaving a bacon slice over and under alternate pieces. Brush with marinade. Broil about 4 inches from heat, basting and turning several times, for 10 to 15 minutes or until bacon is brown and heart no longer pink inside (cut a gash to test). Serve with chile sauce and hot pepper seasoning. Makes 6 to 8 servings.

Braised Stuffed Beef Heart

A whole beef heart is oven-braised to tenderness with a moist and flavorful mushroom and bacon stuffing.

      1   beef heart (about 3 lb.) split lengthwise
          Water
      1   clove garlic, minced or pressed
    ½   cup prepared oil-and-vinegar dressing
          Mushroom stuffing (recipe follows)
      1   cup regular-strength chicken or beef broth
      2   tablespoons *each* all-purpose flour and water, blended smoothly

Trim fat and tubes from heart. Rinse heart and drain well. Add garlic to oil-and-vinegar dressing; pour over heart in a deep bowl. Cover and refrigerate at least 4 hours or overnight, turning several times. Remove heart; discard marinade.

Fill heart with mushroom stuffing; skewer or sew with string to fasten shut. Place heart in a deep, covered casserole; pour in broth. Cover and bake in 325° oven for 3 to 3½ hours or until very tender when pierced. Transfer heart to serving platter; remove fasteners. Pour cooking liquid through wire strainer into a small pan; skim off and discard fat. Add flour paste and bring to a boil, stirring. Slice heart and pass sauce to spoon on individually. Makes 8 to 10 servings.

Mushroom stuffing. In a large frying pan, saute 10 slices bacon, diced, until lightly browned; remove bacon and drain off all but 2 tablespoons of the fat. Return bacon to pan with 1 medium-size onion, finely chopped, and ½ pound mushrooms, sliced; saute, stirring, until mushrooms are limp and all juices have evaporated.

Liver and Bacon Supper Tray with Vegetables

Liver and Bacon
Carrots and Cauliflower
Cherry Tomatoes
Marinated Artichoke Hearts
Finnish Pancake with Peaches (see page 89)

Timing brings together this whole-meal combination featuring liver, bacon, and onions. The onions and bacon are slow-cooked first; next, the carrots and cauliflower boil to tenderness; then at the last moment the liver is browned quickly.

About 4 tablespoons (⅛ lb.) butter or margarine
3 large onions, thinly sliced
½ pound bacon
3 quarts water
1½ pounds calves liver, baby beef liver, or lamb liver, cut in ½-inch-thick slices
All-purpose flour
Salt
12 medium-size carrots
1 medium-size head (about 1½ lb.) cauliflower, leaves removed
Pepper
About 2 tablespoons minced parsley
Cherry tomatoes
1 jar (6 oz.) marinated artichoke hearts, drained (optional)
Lemon wedges

Melt 4 tablespoons of the butter in a wide frying pan over medium-low heat. Add onions and cook, uncovered, stirring frequently, until they are limp, golden, and slightly browned (about 20 minutes). Pour into a bowl; keep warm.

Add bacon slices to frying pan; cook on medium-low heat, uncovered, until brown and crisp. Drain cooked bacon on absorbent material; then transfer to a large platter and keep warm.

Pour from pan all but 3 tablespoons of the bacon drippings; reserve remainder.

In a large kettle, bring water to a boil.

Trim membrane and tubes from liver and cut into strips about 1 inch wide; coat with flour, shaking off excess. Place pieces slightly apart on a pan or waxed paper within easy reach of the range; sprinkle liver with salt.

To boiling water add carrots and 1 teaspoon salt; cover and return to a boil on high heat; cook 3 minutes. Add cauliflower and cook, covered, at boiling for about 10 minutes more, or just until vegetables are easy to pierce with the tip of a sharp knife.

While vegetables cook, return frying pan with bacon drippings to moderately high heat. Add strips of liver (without crowding) and brown quickly on all sides, cooking until no longer pink in center (cut a gash to test; takes about 1½ minutes to a side). Add reserved bacon drippings to pan as needed to prevent sticking. As liver is browned, transfer it to absorbent material to drain briefly; then place on tray with bacon.

When vegetables are cooked, drain and arrange on tray with liver and bacon; dot with butter and sprinkle with salt and pepper. Spoon onions onto liver and sprinkle with parsley. Garnish with cherry tomatoes and artichoke hearts and accompany with lemon wedges to squeeze over individual portions. Makes 6 servings.

Butcher Joe's Beef Heart Soup

In this old farm-family recipe, the beef heart joins a parade of fresh vegetables to make a whole-meal soup.

   1 beef heart (3 to 4 lb.)
     Water
   3 bouillon cubes or 3 teaspoons chicken
       or beef stock base
   1 large onion, chopped
   ½ teaspoon pepper
   1 clove garlic, minced or pressed
   1 bay leaf
   1 tablespoon vinegar
   6 medium-size carrots
   2 stalks celery with leaves
   2 large (about 1 lb.) baking potatoes
   1 small (about 1 lb.) cabbage
   2 large tomatoes
     Salt

Split heart and remove tubes and fat. Rinse heart well and then cut meat into ½-inch cubes. Place in a 5-quart kettle with about 2 quarts water and bouillon cubes, onion, pepper, garlic, bay leaf, and vinegar. Bring to a boil, reduce heat, and simmer, covered, for 2 to 2½ hours or until meat is tender when pierced.

Meanwhile cut carrots in ½-inch pieces; cut celery into ½-inch pieces and coarsely chop the leaves; peel and cut potatoes in 1½-inch chunks; cut cabbage into 8 wedges. Peel tomatoes and cut each into 6 wedges.

When meat is tender, add carrots, celery pieces and leaves, and potatoes to broth. Simmer, covered, for 25 minutes; then add cabbage and tomatoes and cook 10 minutes longer or until all vegetables are tender when pierced. Season to taste with salt before serving. Makes about 4½ quarts (8 or 9 servings of about 2 cups each).

Tripe, Florentine-style

Though tripe is a delicacy in many cuisines, it is one of the least expensive and most neglected meats. To discover some of its potential, try preparing it in the Florentine manner. The tripe is boiled very tender, cut in slivers, blended with a clingingly thick, highly seasoned tomato sauce, and then baked until the flavor of the sauce penetrates the tripe and the top becomes crisp and brown. Crusty bread or mashed potatoes are traditional companions; a green salad is a welcome contrast to the rich flavors.

   1½ pounds plain or honeycomb tripe
    3 quarts water
    2 large onions, minced
    2 cloves garlic, minced
    3 carrots, minced
    6 tablespoons olive oil or salad oil
    1 cup lightly packed minced parsley
    1 large can (1 lb. 13 oz.) tomatoes
    1 can (6 oz.) tomato paste
   ½ teaspoon rosemary leaves
    1 can (14 oz.) or 2 cups regular-strength
        beef broth
      Salt

Rinse tripe and place in a kettle with water. Cover and bring to a boil; simmer for 2 hours or until tripe is very easy to pierce.

Meanwhile, cook onions, garlic, and carrots with oil in a wide frying pan over medium heat, stirring frequently, until vegetables are soft but not browned. Blend in parsley, tomatoes and liquid (breaking tomatoes apart with a spoon), tomato paste, rosemary, and beef broth. Boil, uncovered, stirring occasionally, until quite thick; then stir more frequently, to prevent scorching, until sauce is reduced to 3½ cups. Set aside.

Drain cooked tripe; when cool enough to handle, cut in slivers, ⅛ to ¼ inch wide. Mix tripe with sauce and add salt to taste (at this point mixture can be covered and refrigerated overnight). Spoon tripe into a shallow 2-quart casserole. Bake, uncovered, in a 425° oven for 45 minutes (50 minutes if chilled) or until top gets slightly crusty and browned. Makes 5 or 6 servings.

Boiled Tongue

Serve plain tongue sliced, hot or cold, for a simple entree or for sandwiches. Or, taking advantage of the exceptional affinity this meat has for a wide variety of seasonings, try it with sauces as suggested in the following recipes. Start with a fresh (not corned or smoked) beef tongue or several lamb tongues, whichever is the better value when you shop.

   3 to 3½-pound beef tongue or 3 to 3½
       pounds lamb tongues
   1 large onion, cut in chunks
   2 bay leaves
   6 whole cloves
   1 teaspoon salt
     Water

Rinse tongue well in cool water; then place in a deep, close-fitting kettle. Add onion, bay, cloves, salt, and enough water just to cover meat. Bring to a boil, cover, and simmer gently for about 3 hours for beef tongue or 1½ hours for lamb tongues; tongue should be very tender when pierced. Let cool in broth, then lift out tongue and strip off and discard exterior skin. Use a knife to remove small bones, gristle, and tubes from base of tongue. (At this point you can chill tongue in broth, covered; then reheat it to serve hot.) Cut beef tongue across the grain into ¼-inch-thick slanting slices. Cut lamb tongues into ¼-inch-thick lengthwise slices. Serve hot or cold. Reserve tongue cooking broth for use in following recipes or soup. Makes 8 to 10 servings.

Tongue Provencal

Tomato sauce enriched by onions, herbs, and green peppers, in which cooked tongue simmers, gives this dish the Provencal touch.

> 2 tablespoons olive oil or salad oil
> 1 large onion, chopped
> 1 large green or red bell pepper, seeded and chopped
> 1 clove garlic, minced or pressed
> 2 cans (8 oz. *each*) tomato sauce
> ½ teaspoon thyme leaves
> Boiled tongue, sliced, and ½ cup tongue cooking broth (page 42)

Pour oil into a large frying pan. Add onion, pepper, and garlic. Cook over medium heat, stirring, until vegetables are soft. Blend in tomato sauce, thyme, tongue, and broth. Simmer gently, covered, for about 30 minutes to blend flavors. Makes 8 to 10 servings.

Tongue Baked with Raisin Sauce

The fruit is a sweet and mellow complement to this richly flavored meat.

> Boiled tongue, sliced, and 1 cup tongue cooking broth (page 42)
> ¾ cup raisins or currants
> ½ cup catsup
> 1 medium-size onion, finely chopped
> 1 clove garlic, minced or pressed
> 1 tablespoon Worcestershire
> Minced parsley

Arrange tongue slices, overlapping evenly, in a shallow casserole (about 2-qt. size).

In a small pan combine broth, raisins, catsup, onion, garlic, and Worcestershire. Boil rapidly, stirring, until reduced to 1½ cups. Pour sauce over tongue. Bake, uncovered, in a 350° oven for about 40 minutes or until bubbling. Spoon sauce over meat occasionally while it bakes. Sprinkle with parsley. Makes 8 to 10 servings.

Tongue with Green Sauce

A pungent herb sauce covers slices of hot tongue, in the French fashion.

> 1 tablespoon drained and minced capers
> ½ cup *each* minced parsley and minced onion
> 1 clove garlic, minced or pressed
> ½ teaspoon tarragon leaves, crumbled
> ½ teaspoon salt
> ½ cup olive oil or salad oil
> 2 tablespoons wine vinegar
> Boiled tongue, sliced, and 1 cup tongue cooking broth (page 42)

Stir together capers, parsley, onion, garlic, tarragon, salt, oil, and vinegar; cover and let stand at room temperature for at least 1 hour for flavors to blend.

Place sliced tongue in a wide frying pan and add broth. Slowly heat to a simmer. Lift tongue from liquid to a serving dish and accompany with sauce. (Broth can be used to make soup.) Makes 8 to 10 servings.

Tongue Salad

Accompany with hard-cooked eggs, cauliflowerets, sliced green peppers, and bread and butter for a cold supper tray.

(Recipe continued on next page)

...Tongue Salad (cont'd.)

Boiled tongue (page 42)
½ cup packed coarsely chopped parsley
2 cloves garlic
½ cup salad oil
½ cup vinegar
⅓ cup catsup
½ teaspoon salt
¼ teaspoon pepper

Cut tongue in matchstick pieces. In a blender combine parsley, garlic, oil, vinegar, catsup, salt, and pepper. Whirl until relatively smooth. Mix sauce thoroughly with meat; cover and chill at least 2 hours or as long as several days. Makes 8 to 10 servings.

Mustard and Currant Glazed Tongue

A hefty measure of mustard adds the zip to this jelly-based glaze.

Boiled tongue, sliced, and 1 cup tongue
cooking broth (page 42)
½ cup red currant jelly
⅓ cup Dijon mustard
½ teaspoon ground ginger
1 small onion, minced

Arrange tongue slices, overlapping evenly, in a shallow casserole (about 2-qt. size). In a small pan combine broth, jelly, mustard, ginger, and onion. Bring to a boil and cook, stirring, until reduced to 1½ cups. Pour sauce evenly over tongue. Bake uncovered in a 350° oven for about 40 minutes or until bubbling; baste meat occasionally with juices. Makes 8 to 10 servings.

German-style Sour Kidneys

With gusto, the Germans make this savory stew of beef kidneys, onions, and mushrooms, steeped in a piquant vermouth-flavored sauce.

2 pounds (or about 2) beef kidneys
1 bay leaf
Salt and water
3 tablespoons butter or margarine
1 medium-size onion, thinly sliced
½ pound mushrooms, sliced
1½ teaspoons sugar
2 tablespoons vinegar
2 tablespoons all-purpose flour
⅓ cup dry vermouth or all-purpose Sherry
1 cup regular-strength chicken or beef broth
2 tablespoons catsup
¼ teaspoon thyme leaves
Hot cooked noodles

Cut away fatty membrane from kidneys; cut kidneys in ¼-inch-thick slices. Place in a small pan with bay leaf and add enough salted water to cover generously. Bring to a boil and then simmer gently for 5 minutes. Drain, discard bay, rinse kidneys with cool water, and set aside.

In a wide frying pan, melt 1 tablespoon of the butter. Add onion and mushrooms and cook, stirring, over moderately high heat until vegetables are limp and juices have evaporated. Remove from pan and set aside.

Sprinkle sugar in frying pan and place over high heat until sugar melts and turns a deep amber color. Immediately pour in vinegar and add remaining 2 tablespoons butter; boil, stirring, until most liquid has evaporated.

Add kidneys to pan, blend in flour, then add vermouth, broth, vegetables, catsup, and thyme and bring to a boil, stirring; cook until sauce is thickened slightly. Salt if needed. Serve kidneys in the sauce to spoon over noodles. Makes 6 to 8 servings.

Skewered Veal Kidneys

Broiled on skewers to keep them flat, mild veal kidneys are served with a delicate lemon-parsley butter. The secret of preparing kidneys this way is to cook them just until firm (most of the interior pink color has disappeared); overcooked they become hard and dry.

6 veal kidneys, about 4 oz. *each*
2 or 3 tablespoons melted butter or margarine
6 tablespoons soft butter or margarine
2 tablespoons minced parsley
1 teaspoon grated lemon peel
Salt
Lemon wedges

Cut fatty membrane out of each kidney and split kidneys lengthwise. Thread 1 or 2 kidney halves on each skewer, arranging to keep kidneys secure and flat (loose ends curl when heated). Broil on a rack about 3 inches from heat, 5 to 6 minutes to a side for firm, moist kidneys; baste occasionally with melted butter.

Meanwhile, blend soft butter with parsley and lemon peel.

To serve, remove kidneys from skewers, salt, and accompany with fresh lemon wedges and lemon-parsley butter. Makes 6 servings.

Frankfurter Enchiladas

A wrapping of corn tortillas and a chile-laden sauce give the humble hot dog an intriguing Mexican touch.

    1 medium-size onion, chopped
    2 tablespoons butter or margarine
    2 cans (8 oz. *each*) tomato sauce
    1 can (4 oz.) California green chiles,
         seeded and chopped
    2 teaspoons chile powder
   10 corn tortillas
   10 frankfurters
  1½ cups shredded Cheddar or Swiss cheese

In a frying pan, saute onion in butter until soft. Add tomato sauce, chiles, and chile powder. Bring to a boil, reduce heat, and simmer for about 10 minutes.

Using tongs, dip each tortilla into the hot sauce, roll the tortilla around a frankfurter and arrange, seam down, in a shallow 9 by 13-inch baking pan. When all enchiladas are in the pan, pour over remaining tomato sauce. Sprinkle with shredded cheese.

Bake, uncovered, in a 350° oven for about 25 minutes or until bubbling. Makes 5 servings.

Curried Sausage Supper

The vegetables are kept tender crisp, as in stir-frying, and curry powder gives a bit of spicy heat to this quick sausage dish. Choose from several kinds of sausage: bratwurst, frankfurters, kielbasa (or Polish), or garlic. Applesauce is an accompaniment. Salad, bread, and a light dessert such as sherbet complete the meal.

About 1½ pounds fully cooked sausages
     (suggestions precede)
  ¼ cup (⅛ lb.) butter or margarine
    4 teaspoons curry powder
    1 medium-size mild white onion, cut in
         1-inch squares
    1 medium-size green pepper, seeds removed,
         cut in 1-inch squares
    2 medium-size tomatoes, cut in wedges
    1 can (1 lb.) applesauce

Cut sausage links on the diagonal in ½-inch-thick slices; set aside. Melt butter in a large frying pan over medium heat; stir in curry powder, mixing well. Then add onion and green pepper and cook, stirring, until vegetables are tender crisp (about 2 minutes). Add sausages and continue to cook until meat is heated through and lightly browned (4 minutes longer). Add tomato wedges and stir gently for 1 minute. Pour into a serving dish and accompany with applesauce. Makes about 6 servings.

Cumin Cabbage and Sausages

Speed is the big benefit of cooking with heat-and-eat sausages. In this recipe, kielbasa (or Polish) sausage, garlic franks, or smoked-flavored link sausages top a cabbage and apple combination simmered with cumin, tomato sauce, and mustard. Add pumpernickel bread or boiled potatoes with parsley butter to round out the meal.

    1 large (1½ to 2 lb.) cabbage
    2 tablespoons butter or margarine
    2 teaspoons ground cumin seed
  ½ teaspoon salt
  ⅛ teaspoon pepper
    1 can (8 oz.) tomato sauce
    1 teaspoon Dijon mustard
    2 medium-size red apples (unpeeled),
         finely diced
  1½ pounds fully cooked sausage

Wash cabbage and finely shred (you should have about 10 cups); discard core. Melt butter in a kettle over medium heat; add cabbage and cook, stirring, until it is limp. Stir in cumin, salt, pepper, tomato sauce, mustard, and apples. Cover and simmer for 15 minutes. Arrange sausages on top, cover, and cook 10 minutes longer or until sausages are hot.

To serve, spoon cabbage and apples in the center of a rimmed serving plate; arrange sausages around cabbage. Makes about 6 servings.

The Bargain Birds

Chicken and turkey have earned the title "bargain birds" for good reason. Despite market fluctuations, they continue to be among the best values from the meat counter.

And from the cook's point of view, there is no end to what you can do to give chicken and turkey a fresh look and taste. The recipes in this chapter—with their variety of seasonings and preparation methods—prove the point.

This chapter offers information on how to make regular-strength broth (page 51) from chicken (or turkey). The broth is used liberally throughout this book to add flavor to many dishes. You also learn the practical art of boning a chicken. Buying suggestions are here, too, along with information on storing the meat. The selection of tasty entrees that use cooked meat may make the term "leftover chicken" or "leftover turkey" obsolete in your house. Another economy note in this chapter acquaints you with whole turkey, turkey parts, and ground turkey.

With the recipes and suggestions here, frequent meals with poultry become much more a deliberate adventure than a last resort.

Chicken in Mole Sauce

When served with condiments and rice, the mole makes a whole meal. Accompany with warm, buttered corn tortillas and sangria or beer. Fresh pineapple, if well priced, makes a good dessert.

2 broiler-fryer chickens, *each* about 3 pounds, cut in pieces
1 large onion, sliced
3 whole cloves garlic
1 can (about 14 oz.) or 1¾ cups regular-strength chicken broth
  Mole sauce (directions follow)
2 tablespoons chopped coriander or parsley
¼ cup sesame seed
  Hot cooked rice
  Vegetable condiments (directions follow)
3 limes, cut in wedges

Rinse chicken pieces and pat dry. Place all the chicken but breasts and giblets (reserve giblets for other uses) in a deep kettle. Add onion, garlic, and broth. Cover and simmer 25 minutes. Add breasts to pan; continue to simmer, covered, for 20 minutes or until breasts have lost all pink color in the thickest portions (cut a gash to test).

Lift chicken from broth and set aside to cool slightly; then pull off and discard skin and bones (can be reserved for Chicken Broth, page 51). Cut each breast into 6 pieces; cut any other large pieces into portions the size of the breast meat.

Pour broth through a wire strainer and reserve; discard vegetables. Skim off and discard fat. Measure broth; if less than 3 cups, add water to make that much; if more than 3 cups, boil to reduce to that amount. Reserve for mole sauce. If made ahead, cover and chill chicken and broth separately.

Bring mole sauce to a simmer; add chicken and continue to simmer until meat is hot. Transfer the mole to a serving dish and sprinkle with coriander and sesame seed. Spoon mole onto rice and top with your choice of vegetable condiments. Squeeze on lime to taste. Makes 6 to 8 servings.

Mole sauce. In a blender combine 2 tablespoons chile powder, ¼ cup blanched almonds, ¼ cup diced green-tipped bananas, 1 teaspoon *each* ground cinnamon and salt, 2 corn tortillas (torn in pieces), 2 tablespoons sesame seed, and 1 tablespoon pine nuts (optional). Add enough of the reserved 3 cups chicken broth (see preceding) to help mixture blend to a smooth paste. Pour paste into a pan, add remaining broth, 6 tablespoons butter or margarine, and 1 ounce (1 square) semisweet chocolate. Bring to a simmer, stirring. If made ahead, cover and chill, then reheat.

(For more authentic mole, you can use 2 tablespoons pasilla chile powder instead of regular chile powder, and ½ of a 3.3-oz.-size cake of Mexican beverage chocolate instead of the semisweet chocolate. These ingredients are available in Mexican groceries or delicatessens.)

Vegetable condiments. Place each of the following in individual dishes: 4 medium-size tomatoes, chopped; 1 cup chopped coriander or parsley; 6 green onions, thinly sliced (include some of the tops); about 1½ cups sliced radishes; and ⅓ cup minced canned California green chiles (with seeds and pith removed).

Braised Chicken with Vegetables

Stuffed chicken is browned over direct heat, then baked in its own juices. Onions and potatoes cook along with the bird, absorbing as well as augmenting the good flavors. Serve with an escarole salad.

4-pound broiler-fryer or roasting chicken
  Salt and pepper
¼ pound bulk pork sausage
1 slice firm white bread, broken into coarse crumbs
1 tablespoon minced parsley
3 tablespoons butter or margarine
8 small white boiling onions, peeled
2 medium-size new potatoes, peeled and cut in ½-inch cubes
¼ teaspoon *each* marjoram leaves, oregano leaves, and thyme leaves
1 teaspoon *each* cornstarch and water

Rinse chicken, including giblets; pat dry. Chop chicken liver and set aside. Sprinkle salt and pepper inside chicken cavities. In a kettle with a tight-fitting lid (that can go in the oven), cook sausage until brown and crumbly. Remove sausage with a slotted spoon and drain well. Discard fat in pan. In a bowl combine sausage, bread crumbs, parsley, and chopped liver; stuff into body cavity of chicken. Skewer cavity closed; tie drumsticks together. Turn bird over and skewer neck skin to back; secure wings akimbo.

In same kettle, melt butter over moderate heat; put in chicken and giblets and brown well on all sides (takes about 25 minutes). Add onions and potatoes during last 10 minutes; stir to brown evenly. Sprinkle evenly with marjoram, oregano, and thyme.

Bake, covered, in a 300° oven for about 1 hour or until leg jiggles easily.

(Recipe continued on next page)

To serve, place chicken on platter; remove vegetables with a slotted spoon and arrange around chicken. Keep warm. Remove giblets and chop; set aside.

To make gravy, skim fat from pan juices. Blend cornstarch with water until smooth, add to pan, and cook, stirring, until thickened. Add chopped giblets. Pour gravy into a small serving bowl and pass to spoon over chicken and vegetables. Makes 4 servings.

Chicken with Sweet Onions

Sauteed onions, spiced Moroccan-style, top roasted chicken pieces.

¼ cup slivered almonds (optional)
  3-pound broiler-fryer chicken, cut in pieces
  Salt, pepper, and paprika
¼ cup (⅛ lb.) butter or margarine
4 or 5 large onions, thinly sliced
2 tablespoons firmly packed brown sugar
½ teaspoon ground cinnamon
  Lemon wedges

Spread almonds in a single layer in a shallow pan. Bake in a 400° oven, stirring often, 5 to 10 minutes or until golden. Set aside.

Rinse chicken pieces and pat dry. Sprinkle with salt, pepper, and paprika. Arrange pieces side by side, skin side up, in a shallow baking pan. Bake in a 400° oven for about 50 minutes or until pieces are well browned.

Meanwhile, melt butter in a 10 to 12-inch frying pan over medium heat. Add onions, separating into rings, and cook slowly, stirring often, until onions are limp and golden (about 30 minutes). The onions should not show signs of browning during the first 15 minutes; if they do, reduce heat. Sprinkle in the brown sugar and cinnamon and stir to blend.

Place chicken pieces on a serving plate and cover with the cooked onions. Sprinkle with toasted almonds. Serve with lemon wedges to squeeze over chicken. Makes 4 servings.

Oven Orange Chicken

Fresh orange slices are a refreshing and attractive part of this chicken casserole. Accompany with bulgur wheat pilaf or brown rice.

  3-pound broiler-fryer chicken, cut in pieces
¼ cup all-purpose flour
½ teaspoon garlic salt
⅛ teaspoon pepper
2 tablespoons salad oil
¼ cup *each* finely chopped onion and green pepper
½ cup tomato-based chile sauce or catsup
1 teaspoon prepared mustard
2 tablespoons soy sauce
1 cup orange juice
3 large oranges, peeled with a knife and sliced crosswise

Rinse chicken pieces and pat dry. Combine flour, garlic salt, and pepper. Coat chicken pieces in flour mixture, shaking off excess. Heat oil in a large frying pan over medium heat; add chicken and brown on all sides; transfer to a shallow 3-quart casserole.

To the frying pan add onion and green pepper and saute until limp. Stir in chile sauce, mustard, soy, and ¾ cup of the orange juice. Bring to a full, rolling boil. Pour sauce over chicken; cover.

Bake in a 350° oven for 30 minutes. Uncover and bake 25 minutes longer or until thigh meat is no longer pink near bone (cut to test). Transfer to a rimmed platter; decorate with orange slices. Skim off and discard fat from sauce; stir in remaining orange juice and then pour over chicken. Makes 4 servings.

A Whole Chicken Pays Off

It really pays to bone your chicken when you want the boneless pieces for such special dishes as the saute dish or the leg roasts (both on page 49). And even when you want just parts of the chicken, it is economical to buy the whole thing.

The price of chicken changes, but the relativity of the saving does not. Typically, breasts are about twice as much per pound as whole chicken. If you buy chicken breasts at $1.28 a pound, the completely waste-free meat (no bones or skin) costs $2.05 a pound. If you purchase a whole chicken at 64¢ a pound, the completely waste-free meat it yields (no bones or skin) will cost $1.70 a pound and will represent about 37 percent of the total weight of the bird.

In addition to this saving of 20 percent on the cost of the boneless meat, *you get the bonus* of two wings, the giblets and neck, and all the bones, skin, and fat. Each of these can be used effectively in other dishes or in Chicken Broth (page 51).

For 2 cups of boned, skinned, raw chicken (about 1 lb. 4 oz.), you need to start with a 3-pound broiler-fryer.

Basic Chicken Saute

Boneless chicken pieces, pounded thin and sauteed quickly, become fork tender, are exceptionally moist, and have a flavor quite similar to that of more costly veal. You can season the chicken in a number of ways, making this basic recipe one to use again and again.

3½ to 4-pound broiler-fryer chicken, boned
    as directed on page 50
    Salt and pepper
3 to 4 tablespoons butter or margarine (may
    be part salad oil)
    Seasoning liquid (suggestions follow)
¼ cup whipping cream
    Garnish (optional; suggestions follow)

Use only the boneless, skinned piece of the chicken. Cut breast in half lengthwise; cut legs apart at knee section. Spread chicken pieces out, cut side down, about 5 to 6 inches apart on clear plastic wrap; tuck any scraps of meat under the big pieces. Cover with another piece of plastic wrap. Pound with a flat-surfaced mallet until each portion is uniformly no more than ⅛-inch-thick.

(At this point, you can fold meat up in the plastic wrap, slip into a plastic bag, and refrigerate as long as 24 hours.)

Sprinkle meat lightly with salt and pepper.

In a 10 to 12-inch frying pan, melt 2 tablespoons of the butter over medium-high heat. Add dark meat and cook, turning once, until slightly browned (takes 2 to 3 minutes). Push meat to one side of pan, adding more butter if needed to prevent sticking. Add breast portions and cook until edges turn paler in color; then turn and continue to cook until slightly browned (takes 2 to 3 minutes). Add seasoning liquid to pan and bring to a boil. Set pan off heat while you lift out meat and transfer to a serving dish; keep warm.

Return pan to highest heat and add cream; boil rapidly, stirring, until large, shiny bubbles form. Drain any juices from chicken into sauce. If desired, stir in a garnish and heat through. Spoon sauce over chicken and serve. Makes 3 or 4 servings.

Seasoning liquid. You can use 2 tablespoons lemon juice or 2 or 3 tablespoons broth (chicken or beef), dry white wine, or dry red wine. Or use 3 tablespoons Port, Sherry, or Madeira, or 2 tablespoons of a liqueur such as brandy or Cointreau (or other orange-flavored liqueur), or gin or Scotch whiskey. Set aflame by holding a match close to pan edge as soon as liqueur is added (be sure pan is not beneath a ventilating exhaust or flammable items); shake pan until flame dies.

Garnishes. Stir into pan juices any one of the following: ½ to 1 cup sliced sauteed mushrooms, ¼ to ½ cup toasted or sauteed chopped or sliced almonds, ¾ cup seedless grapes, 2 or 3 tablespoons sauteed chopped shallots or onion, or 1 teaspoon Dijon mustard.

Rosemary Chicken Bundles

Two boned chicken legs, tied together, make a small roast. Assemble the chicken bundles you need; two are just about right for three servings.

2 whole chicken legs
    Salt, pepper
1 clove garlic, minced or pressed
    Olive oil
⅛ teaspoon rosemary leaves (or 1 sprig
    fresh rosemary)

To make each bundle, bone chicken legs (follow Step 5, page 50) but *do not* remove skin. Sprinkle meat with salt, pepper, and garlic; drizzle with olive oil. Scatter rosemary leaves (or lay sprig of rosemary) on inside of one leg. Place meaty sides together, positioning thigh section of one over drumstick section of the other. Pull loose skin from edges of bottom leg up over top leg, tucking in meat from top leg to make a neat bundle. With cord, tie legs together in 3 equidistant places.

Brush bundle with olive oil. Bake, uncovered, in a 400° oven for about 50 minutes or until well browned and meat is no longer pink in center (cut into thickest portion to test). Or you can cook chicken on a grill 4 to 6 inches above a solid bed of glowing coals, turning often, until well browned and no longer pink in center (takes 40 to 50 minutes). Makes 1 large or 2 medium servings.

How to Bone a Chicken

Many elegant dishes begin with boneless pieces of chicken; you can keep the cost down by learning to do the boning yourself. It's not nearly as complex as it seems—with a little practice and a good sharp knife, you can carry out the boning process quickly and smoothly.

1. Rinse chicken; pat dry. With chicken on its back, force each thigh and wing back from body until joints snap free.

Turn chicken breast-down and cut down the center of the back, through the skin. Pull the skin back on each side so you can see where the muscles attach to the bone. At midpoint, where the back curves in dramatically (this spot is called the oyster) cut close to bone with knife, freeing meat from the curve. Continue cutting through the joint and on around to the tail. Cut through skin to separate the leg from the body. Repeat to remove other leg.

2. To remove wings, slip knife tip into wing joints and cut wings free, taking as little meat from the carcass as possible.

3. Working from the back, slip knife along the neck and down around ribs, freeing meat from carcass; you need to cut meat from both sides of the shoulder blade as you go. Continue to cut close to carcass as you free the breast down to the edge of the keel (or breast) bone. At the wishbone, you need to work with the tip of the knife to free as much of the meat as possible. Save all small scraps of the meat; they can be used later. (When it seems simpler, use your fingers to slide between the carcass and meat to release the breast.) Repeat to free the other side.

4. Grasp the breast meat and pull off the carcass. Pull off skin; trim away fat and any of the coarse cartilage from the keel, if it sticks to the breast meat.

5. To bone legs, cut to the bone around the narrow base of drumstick; pull off skin. On the inside of each leg, cut along the entire length to the bone. Then, using the knife, scrape meat free from bone; cut around the joint to release the meat. The long, fibrous, silvery tendons in drumstick do not need to be cut away.

Cut down center of back

Slip knife along ribs and breast bone

Pull breast meat from carcass

Scrape meat from leg bone

Pound boned meat with mallet

Oriental Spiced Chicken Wings

Wings simmer in a rich brown sauce. Serve altogether on hot cooked rice as a main dish, or serve wings with sauce as a dip for an untidy, but tasty, snack or first course.

Sesame oil—a fragrant, golden oil of sesame seed—can add a special flavor to this dish. You may have to shop in an Oriental market to find it, but it is optional.

20 chicken wings (about 4 lb.)
½ cup *each* soy sauce and dry Sherry
6 green onions, thinly sliced
1 chicken bouillon cube or 1 teaspoon chicken stock base
1 cup water
2 teaspoons Chinese five-spice (or ¾ teaspoon ground ginger, ½ teaspoon ground cinnamon, ¼ teaspoon *each* ground allspice and crushed anise seeds, and ⅛ teaspoon ground cloves
1 teaspoon sesame oil (optional)
¼ cup firmly packed brown sugar
2 tablespoons cornstarch
   Hot cooked rice (optional)

Rinse chicken wings and pat dry. If desired, cut off wing tips and reserve for Chicken Broth (see below); cut wings in half at first joint.

In a wide frying pan combine soy sauce, Sherry, half the green onions, bouillon, ¾ cup of the water, five-spice, sesame oil, and brown sugar. Bring to a boil, add wings, cover, and simmer about 25 minutes or until wings are tender when pierced.

Lift out wings and keep warm. Blend cornstarch with remaining ¼ cup water and stir into sauce; bring to a rolling boil, stirring.

To present as a main dish, serve wings in sauce on rice, garnished with remaining green onions.

To serve as an appetizer, have sauce in a small dish and wings alongside, sprinkling some of the reserved green onion onto both; keep warm. Dip wings into sauce as you eat; provide napkins to catch drips. Makes 4 main-dish servings or 8 to 10 appetizer servings.

Chicken and Egg Donburi

Donburi is to the Japanese what an omelet is to the French or what scrambled eggs may be at your house. It's a quick-to-make dish, and because you make one serving at a time, it's ideal when you are cooking for only one or two people.

1 tablespoon salad oil (may be part butter or margarine)
2 or 3 medium-size mushrooms, thinly sliced
   About 3 tablespoons sliced green onion (include part of the tops)
3 to 4 ounces boneless, skinned chicken, cut in bite-size pieces (about ½ breast or 1 thigh)
3 tablespoons regular-strength chicken broth
1 tablespoon Marin (sweet rice wine) or 1 tablespoon dry Sherry with 1 teaspoon sugar
1 tablespoon soy sauce
½ teaspoon ground ginger
1 egg, beaten
¾ to 1 cup hot cooked rice

In a small (about 5-inch) frying pan over medium-high heat, combine oil, mushrooms, and 2 tablespoons of the onion. Cook, stirring, for 1 minute or until vegetables are slightly limp. Add chicken and cook, stirring, for another 1 or 2 minutes or until meat is lightly browned. Add broth, Marin, soy, and ginger; cook, stirring, until only about ⅛ inch of sauce remains in pan.

Reduce heat to low and gradually pour egg over contents of pan. Cover and cook about 1 minute or until egg is just firmed. Spoon rice into a serving bowl. Run a spatula around edge of egg mixture to loosen and slide it from the pan onto rice. Sprinkle with remaining onion. Makes 1 serving.

Chicken Broth

Because this broth is unsalted, you can boil it down for greater flavor concentration if you like; otherwise, use it as you would canned regular-strength chicken broth or reconstituted chicken stock base, adding salt to taste.

When you bone a chicken or have leftovers from a cooked chicken, store up bones and scraps in your freezer, making broth when you have accumulated the carcasses of at least 2 or 3 chickens (may be part or all turkey bones in equivalent proportions).

   Carcasses (or equivalent) of 2 or 3 chickens (including leg bones, fat, skin, wing tips, and also neck, gizzard, heart—if you have no other use for them); use uncooked chicken, or leftover bones, skin, drippings of cooked chicken
   Water
6 to 8 parsley sprigs
2 or 3 small carrots, chopped
2 or 3 small onions, chopped

(Recipe continued on next page)

Place the carcasses (or equivalent) in a deep kettle; bones should fill bottom of pan. Barely cover with water (about 10 to 15 cups for 2 or 3 chickens). Add parsley, carrots, and onions.

Bring to a boil, cover, and simmer about 3 hours. Let stand until lukewarm, then pour through a wire strainer, reserving broth. Discard residue. Chill broth, covered; skim off fat when solidified, if desired. Refrigerate broth up to 4 or 5 days or freeze in portions that are easy to use (such as ice cubes or 2 or 3-cup-size units). Yield from 2 or 3 carcasses is 10 to 15 cups.

cups of the stock and cook, stirring, until thickened. Return to large pan. Beat egg yolks slightly with lemon juice, add some of the hot mixture, then return to pan and remove immediately from heat. Season to taste with salt and pour this liquid over chicken pieces.

Serve in large wide soup bowls; top each serving with lemon slices, minced parsley, and a little ground pepper. Makes 6 to 8 servings.

To make this soup ahead, wait to add egg yolks and lemon mixture until just before serving. Bone chicken pieces if desired.

Le Waterzooi de Volaille

Serve slices of buttered dark bread with this knife-and-fork, lemon and chicken soup from Belgium.

2 broiler-fryer chickens, *each* 3 to 4 pounds, cut in pieces
5 tablespoons butter or margarine
2 cups diced celery
¾ cup sliced leek (white part only)
1 large onion, chopped (or use 2 large onions and omit leek)
8 cups water
About 1½ teaspoons salt
2 sprigs parsley
½ bay leaf
1 sprig thyme or ½ teaspoon thyme leaves
6 whole black peppers
6 tablespoons all-purpose flour
2 egg yolks
3 tablespoons lemon juice
Thin lemon slices
Minced parsley
Coarsely ground pepper

Rinse chicken pieces and pat dry.

Melt 1 tablespoon of the butter in a large kettle. Add celery, leek, and onion. Cook, stirring, until soft but not browned. Add water, 1½ teaspoons salt, parsley sprigs, bay leaf, thyme, and black peppers. Bring to a boil and then simmer, covered, for 30 minutes. Add chicken, except breasts, and giblets (reserve giblets for other purpose) and continue simmering, covered, for 25 minutes; add breasts and simmer 20 minutes or until breasts have lost all pink color throughout (cut a gash to test). Transfer chicken pieces to a large soup tureen and keep warm. Discard bay leaf and parsley sprigs; keep stock simmering.

Melt remaining 4 tablespoons butter in a small pan and blend in flour. Gradually mix in about 4

Basic Simmered Turkey

If you can simmer a chicken for a supply of moist, tender meat, why not do the same with a turkey? As a bonus, this recipe also tells you how to make rich turkey broth from the simmering liquid.

You will need a large kettle—about a 12-quart size for a 12 to 14-pound turkey. Or have the turkey cut into quarters and divide meat and simmering liquid between two kettles.

12 to 14-pound turkey
12 cups (3 qt.) water
1 large carrot, cut in chunks
1 onion, quartered
1 stalk celery, thickly sliced
3 sprigs parsley
6 whole black peppers
1 tablespoon salt

Remove giblets and rinse turkey. Place in a large kettle (at least 12-qt. size) with giblets (except liver). Add water, carrot, onion, celery, parsley, peppers, and salt. Cover and simmer for about 12 to 14 minutes per pound or until thighs are tender (add liver during last 10 minutes). Cool turkey in broth; cover and refrigerate overnight.

Lift turkey from broth and remove skin. Cut each side of breast from bone and lift off whole sections of white meat. Leave sections whole or cut in thin slices, as desired, and set aside.

Cut all remaining meat away from bones in large chunks or cubes and package to suit your plans for serving it; wrap and refrigerate or freeze. Gather up all turkey bones and skin and return to cooking broth in kettle. Cover kettle, heat to a boil, reduce heat, and simmer for 2 hours. Cool, strain, and chill broth; discard bones and seasoning vegetables. When broth is cold, skim off and discard fat. You should have about 10 cups concentrated, bouncy, gelled stock. Turn into freezer containers, cover, label, and freeze.

Siberian Chicken Soup

Siberian Chicken Soup
Hot Mustard   Sour Cream
Green Salad
Bread and Butter
Georgian Tea   Cookies

Unexpected and surprisingly agreeable taste sensations make this Russian-style chicken soup, reputedly of Siberian origin, suitable for both the cautious and the adventurous, and festive enough for a small party.

It's wholesome and sturdy, fragrantly spiced, and loaded with vegetables. You serve it in wide bowls to eat with knife, fork, and spoon, adding hot mustard and, if you like, sour cream for controlled zest and smoothness. A green salad with an oil and vinegar dressing rounds out the main course, along with crusty bread or a dark heavy loaf.

For dessert, brew an aromatic tea (Earl Grey or spiced) and then pass a fruit jam such as strawberry, cherry, or other berry to stir by the spoonful into cups (or into glasses, to be Russian) of tea.

Siberian chicken soup. You can start the soup as much as a day ahead; then as it finishes cooking there is time to organize the rest of the meal.

3½ to 4-pound broiler-fryer chicken, cut
     in serving pieces
    Stewing broth (directions follow)
2 large carrots
1 medium-size (about ½ lb.) celery
    root
3 tablespoons lemon juice
1 teaspoon sugar
¼ cup pearl or long grain rice
1 small can (8 oz.) stewed tomatoes
6 whole allspice
6 whole cardamom pods
¼ teaspoon thyme leaves
1 jar or can (1 lb.) pickled red
    cabbage
    Chopped parsley and lemon wedges
    Hot mustard and sour cream
    Salt and pepper

Add the chicken and giblets to stewing broth in a kettle (reserve liver for other uses), placing breast on top. Bring to a boil, reduce heat to simmering; cover and cook 15 minutes or until breast pieces have lost all pink color throughout (cut a gash to test). Lift out the breast pieces and set aside.

Continue to simmer remaining chicken, cov-

ered, for another 30 minutes or until thighs have lost all pink color and meat pulls easily from bones. Lift all the chicken from stewing broth and place with breast.

When chicken is cool enough to touch, strip off skin and remove bones, keeping meat pieces as large as possible. Return all bones, skin, tiny scraps of meat, and any accumulated juices to the broth. Return broth to a boil, then simmer, covered, for about 1 hour. Chill chicken meat, covered.

Pour broth through a wire strainer, pressing as much liquid as possible from the bony mixture. Discard bones. Skim fat from broth; or chill broth, covered, until ready to complete soup and then lift off and discard fat.

Peel carrots and celery root and cut in about ½-inch cubes. Bring broth to a boil and add vegetables, lemon juice, sugar, rice, tomatoes and liquid (break up tomatoes with a spoon), allspice, seeds from cardamom pods (discard pods), and thyme. Simmer, covered, for about 25 minutes or until vegetables and rice are tender. Stir chicken meat into broth; simmer about 5 minutes more to heat through.

Serve soup from the kettle or a tureen. Have in separate containers the unheated red cabbage, chopped parsley, lemon wedges, mustard, and sour cream. Ladle soup into wide bowls, adding to each a mound of the red cabbage. Sprinkle with parsley, garnish with lemon wedges, and season to taste with salt and pepper. Serve with knife, fork, and spoon. Pass mustard and sour cream to add to soup. Makes 4 or 5 main-dish servings.

Stewing broth. Combine in a kettle 6 cups water, ¼ teaspoon whole coriander seed, seeds from 3 whole cardamom (discard pods), ½ teaspoon whole allspice, ¼ teaspoon whole black pepper, ½ teaspoon thyme leaves, 4 or 5 sprigs parsley, ½ teaspoon salt, 1 large onion, chopped, and 1 large carrot, sliced. Bring to a boil, cover, and simmer 30 minutes, then use according to directions.

How Much Meat Do You Get from a Turkey?

A cooked 12 to 14-pound turkey will yield 2 to 2½ pounds of breast meat perfect for slicing, and about 8 cups of scrappier pieces suitable for cubing or dicing. In total, you have enough for 6 to 8 servings of white meat when used for a cold meat platter, sandwiches, salads, or a casserole.

The dark meat is enough for about 8 servings when added to soups, made into turkey pie, or made into creamed or curried dishes. The cooked giblets may be diced and added to dark meat.

Roast Turkey with Garlic Baste

A roast turkey may be "the holiday bird," but for everyday occasions it can also be the source of a large supply of versatile, economical, ready-to-eat meat. Roast a turkey any day; serve part of it for dinner and keep part of it in the refrigerator or freezer to have on hand for salads, sandwiches, casseroles, and many other dishes. Here we tell you how to roast it (starting the turkey with the breast down to assure you of moister meat), basting either with butter or with a pungent garlic-and-paprika baste.

1 hen or tom turkey
　Garlic basting sauce (recipe follows), or
　¼ cup melted butter or margarine

Remove neck and giblets, rinse turkey inside and out, and pat dry.

Brush butter or basting sauce all over turkey and inside body cavity. Fold wings akimbo; do not secure legs.

Place turkey breast-down on a rack in a shallow pan. Bake, uncovered, in a 325° oven. Allow 15 minutes per pound for hens up to 15 pounds, 12 minutes per pound for toms weighing 16 pounds and over.

When turkey is about half done, remove from oven and, with your hands (protected by paper towels), turn bird onto its back. Insert a meat thermometer into thickest portion of thigh, making sure it is not touching bone, and continue to cook until meat thermometer registers 180° to 185°. Drumstick should move easily when jiggled and thigh meat should feel soft when pinched. Brush occasionally throughout cooking time, using melted butter or remaining garlic baste. Allow about 1 pound turkey for each serving. Serve hot or cold.

Garlic basting sauce. Blend 6 cloves garlic, minced or pressed, with 1 tablespoon paprika, ½ teaspoon salt, ¼ teaspoon pepper, and ¼ cup salad oil.

Turkey Cannelloni

When you're called upon to feed a crowd, a turkey is an economical way to begin. Here, a 12 to 14-pound bird and 2 pounds of cooked ham are the starting point for enough deliciously filled and sauced crepes to serve 40 people. A huge green salad and bread and butter complete a main course.

If you are cooking by committee you can divide the chores into these steps: 1) Roast turkey; 2) Make filling; 3) Cook crepes; 4) Make tomato sauce; 5) Prepare cream sauce; 6) Slice cheese; 7) Assemble; 8) Bake and serve.

12 to 14-pound turkey (including giblets), roasted with butter baste according to directions at left and then cooled; reserve fat-free drippings
　2 pounds boneless cooked ham
　2 pounds cottage cheese
　2 cups shredded Parmesan cheese
　6 eggs
½ teaspoon ground nutmeg
5½ teaspoons salt
¾ cup (⅜ lb.) butter or margarine
　1 cup all-purpose flour, unsifted
　3 quarts milk
　2 cups regular-strength chicken broth or turkey broth
1½ teaspoons salt
　Tomato sauce (recipe follows)
　Crepes (directions follow)
　4 pounds jack cheese, thinly sliced

Peel skin from cooked turkey and strip all meat from carcass. (Save skin and bones for making broth, page 51.)

Cut turkey pieces and ham into small chunks. Grind through the fine blade of a food chopper the turkey, ham, cottage cheese, and Parmesan cheese. Mix the turkey drippings and eggs thoroughly with the ground meats and cheese. Season meat with nutmeg and 4 teaspoons of the salt. Chill, covered, until ready to use (overnight if convenient). Makes about 20 cups.

In a pan (about 6-qt.), melt butter and blend in flour, stirring until lightly browned. Gradually stir in milk and broth and add remaining 1½ teaspoons salt. Bring cream sauce to a boil, stirring frequently; then simmer slowly for about 20 minutes. Add tomato sauce and simmer 5 or 10 minutes longer. Cool and chill, covered, until ready to use (overnight if you wish).

To assemble cannelloni, spoon ¼ cup of the ground meat filling along the center of each crepe and roll crepe around filling. Repeat process until all meat is used. Place cannelloni seam side down in shallow baking pans (you will need 4 pans, each 11 by 17 inches, or ones with equivalent areas). At this point you can cover and chill cannelloni for as long as 24 hours.

Ladle cream sauce mixture evenly over filled cannelloni. Top sauce with sliced cheese. Bake in a 400° oven for 20 to 25 minutes or until cheese is melted and sauce is bubbling. Use a wide spatula to lift cannelloni onto dinner plates. Allow 2 cannelloni for each serving. Makes about 80 cannelloni, or 40 servings.

Tomato sauce. Melt ¼ cup (⅛ lb.) butter or margarine in a pan. Add 2 large onions, chopped; cook, stirring, until soft. Stir in 1 can (1 lb. 12 oz.) tomatoes and juice, breaking the tomatoes into large chunks. Season with 2 teaspoons basil leaves and ½ teaspoon salt; simmer for 15 minutes. Add, hot or cooled, to cream sauce.

Crepes. Make 6 times the recipe for crepes on page 37. You need 80 crepes.

Ways to Defrost a Frozen Turkey

You can defrost a frozen whole turkey in one of three ways, depending on your time schedule and refrigerator space.

To defrost a turkey in the refrigerator, place the bird in a pan with the plastic wrap punctured or partially opened. Leave the turkey in the refrigerator; allow 2 to 4 days (or about 24 hours for each 6 pounds of turkey) for it to thaw.

To thaw a turkey at room temperature, place the unopened plastic-wrapped turkey in a large paper bag and set aside. Allow about 1 hour per pound for thawing.

To thaw turkey in a hurry, immerse the unopened plastic-wrapped bird in cool water; change the water frequently. Allow about 30 minutes per pound of turkey.

It is preferable to cook a fresh or thawed turkey promptly. However, you can keep a thawed, ready-to-cook turkey for 2 to 3 days in a refrigerator: take off the plastic bag, remove the giblets and neck, and then cover the turkey with a damp cloth and refrigerate until ready to roast; keep the cloth damp. Don't stuff the turkey until ready to roast.

Turkey Tarragon Scalloppini

Half of a boned 4-pound turkey breast makes the right amount for this saute dish. The sliced meat, pounded thin for quick cooking, is moist and fork tender.

> About 1½ pounds boned and skinned
>   turkey breast
> About ¼ cup all-purpose flour
> About 5 tablespoons butter or margarine
> ¼ pound mushrooms, sliced
> 1 tablespoon finely chopped parsley
> ½ teaspoon *each* salt and crushed tarragon
>   leaves
> ⅛ teaspoon pepper
> ⅓ cup dry vermouth

Slice turkey across the grain into ½-inch-thick slices; lay them between sheets of plastic wrap and pound firmly but gently with a flat-surfaced mallet until slices are uniformly ¼ inch thick. Coat meat with flour, shake off excess.

Melt about half the butter in a large frying pan over medium-high heat; add turkey slices without crowding and cook until just lightly browned on each side (about 4 minutes total). As pieces are cooked, transfer to a serving dish; keep warm.

(Recipe continued on next page)

Melt remaining butter in pan, add mushrooms, and cook until they are limp (about 5 minutes). Stir in parsley, salt, tarragon, pepper, and vermouth; boiling rapidly, stir to incorporate brown bits clinging to pan. Pour evenly over turkey and serve. Makes 4 to 6 servings.

Ground Turkey?

One economical form of poultry that appears with increasing frequency in the meat case of the supermarket is ground turkey. Like ground beef, it is raw meat (boneless turkey parts), ground, packaged, and sold by weight. It is a mild meat that lends itself to a variety of flavorings (for ideas on how to serve ground turkey, see below).

Turkey and Green Chile Tumble

You spoon the hot, seasoned turkey into crisp lettuce leaves and eat out of hand. The contrast of hot and cold, crisp and saucy is intriguing. This can be a casual entree for two.

¾ pound ground turkey
1 egg white
2 tablespoons dry Sherry
1 teaspoon *each* sugar and cornstarch
1 teaspoon soy sauce
1 clove garlic, minced or pressed
2 tablespoons salad oil
4 to 6 tablespoons finely chopped, seeded, canned California green chiles
1 tablespoon grated fresh ginger root or 1 teaspoon ground ginger
Sauce (directions follow)
4 green onions, thinly sliced (tops included)
About 35 small butter lettuce or romaine leaves, washed
About 1 cup chopped coriander or parsley (optional)

Mix turkey with egg white, Sherry, sugar, cornstarch, soy, and garlic.

Heat oil in a large frying pan over high heat. Add turkey mixture, chiles, and ginger; cook, stirring, until meat is no longer pink (3 to 4 minutes). Add sauce and green onions; cook, stirring, until sauce thickens and boils (about 1 minute).

Pour meat mixture into a serving dish and accompany with separate containers of lettuce and coriander.

To eat, spoon a little hot turkey mixture onto a lettuce leaf, top with a little coriander, roll up,

and eat. Makes about 35 appetizers or 2 main-dish servings.

Sauce. Stir together 1 teaspoon cornstarch, ½ teaspoon salt, 1 tablespoon *each* water and dry Sherry, and 2 teaspoons soy sauce.

Turkey Bacon Logs

A crisp bacon wrapping enhances these juicy turkey patties; serve them for breakfast, for dinner, or to go into sandwiches like a hamburger.

1 pound ground turkey
¼ cup fine dry bread crumbs
1 egg
¼ cup *each* minced parsley and green onion (including some of the tops)
¼ teaspoon *each* salt and pepper
8 slices bacon

Thoroughly mix together the turkey, crumbs, egg, parsley, onion, salt, and pepper. Divide into 8 equal portions and shape each into a 2-inch-long log. Wrap each log with 1 slice of bacon; secure ends with picks. Place logs slightly apart on a rack in a shallow pan. Bake in a 425° oven until bacon is brown and crisp, about 40 minutes. Makes 4 servings.

Cooked Meat to Spare

When chickens are a bargain, why not buy two and cook them at the same time? You can serve one for dinner; the second will give you an extra supply of cooked meat to have on hand. A cooked, boned, and skinned 3 to 3½-pound broiler-fryer chicken yields about 2 cups of moist, tender meat for casseroles, salads, and sandwiches.

Mexican Lasagna

If more convenient, you can prepare this casserole early in the day or the night before; then just slip it into the oven when it's time to heat and serve.

    2 tablespoons salad oil
    1 large onion, chopped
    2 cloves garlic, minced or pressed
    1 red or green bell pepper, seeded and
        chopped
    2 cans (10¾ oz. *each*) condensed tomato
        soup
    1 can (10 oz.) enchilada sauce
    1 teaspoon salt
    ½ teaspoon pepper
    2 teaspoons chile powder
    1 teaspoon ground cumin seed
    1 package (10 oz.) lasagne, cooked and
        drained according to package directions
      Cheese filling (directions follow)
    4 cups cooked chicken or turkey, torn into
        large pieces (skin and bones removed)
    6 ounces *each* sliced sharp Cheddar cheese
        and jack cheese

In a large frying pan, heat oil; add onion, garlic, and green pepper. Cook, stirring often, over medium heat until onion is limp. Add soup, enchilada sauce, salt, pepper, chile powder, and cumin. Simmer, uncovered, about 10 minutes or until thickened; stir often to prevent sticking.

Cover the bottom of a shallow 3½ to 4-quart casserole with half of the cooked lasagne noodles. Spread half the cheese filling over the noodles, then top with half the sauce. Arrange half the cooked meat over the sauce and half the sliced cheese. Repeat layers to use all remaining noodles, cheese filling, sauce, meat, and sliced cheese. At this point you can cover and chill the casserole.

Bake, covered, in a 375° oven for 35 minutes (50 minutes, if chilled) or until bubbling. Let stand, uncovered, about 5 minutes before cutting into rectangles. Serve portions, using a wide spatula. Makes 10 to 12 servings.

Cheese filling. Stir together 1 pint (2 cups) small curd creamed cottage cheese, 2 eggs, ⅓ cup chopped parsley, and 3 to 4 tablespoons diced canned California green chiles.

Citrus Chicken Salad

Orange peel flavors the dressing, and orange slices accompany the salad.

    1 teaspoon grated orange peel
    ¾ cup thinly sliced celery
    ⅓ cup *each* chopped green pepper and green
        onion
    ½ cup *each* sour cream and mayonnaise
    1 tablespoon *each* lemon juice and sugar
      About 3 cups bite-size pieces cooked
        chicken or turkey (skin and bones
        removed)
      Salt and pepper
    2 large oranges
      Lettuce leaves
    ½ cup coarsely chopped salted peanuts or
        salted almonds

Blend orange peel, celery, green pepper, green onion, sour cream, mayonnaise, lemon juice, sugar, and meat. Season salad with salt and pepper to taste; cover and chill at least 1 hour or as long as 24 hours.

Peel oranges, cutting away white membrane; then cut fruit in thin crosswise slices. Line a serving dish with lettuce, top with salad, and surround with oranges. Sprinkle salad with nuts. Makes 4 servings.

Curried Turkey and Potato Salad

Chunks of turkey and waxy-textured new potatoes chill in a sweet-tart curry dressing to make this hearty salad.

    3 cups diced, hot, cooked new potatoes
      Curry dressing (recipe follows)
    3 cups cubed cooked turkey or chicken
        (skin and bones removed)
    1½ cups thinly sliced celery
    ¼ cup thinly sliced green onion (include
        some tops)
    2 hard-cooked eggs, coarsely chopped
    2 tablespoons finely chopped mint (or dried
        mint, crumbled) or parsley
      Lettuce leaves
      Thinly sliced green pepper rings

Put potatoes in a salad bowl and mix with dressing. Gently stir in meat, celery, onion, eggs, and mint. Cover and refrigerate until cold or as long as 24 hours. To serve, garnish with lettuce and green pepper. Makes 4 to 6 servings.

Curry dressing. Blend ¾ cup mayonnaise, ½ teaspoon salt, ⅛ teaspoon pepper, 1 teaspoon *each* curry powder and brown or Dijon mustard, and 2 tablespoons *each* sweet pickle relish and wine vinegar.

Sensible Savings with Seafood

At least half of this chapter contains recipes flexible enough to let you take advantage of the best buys when you shop for fish. They call for any mild, firm, white-fleshed fish — sometimes fillets, sometimes steaks (often it's the dimension of the piece that is more important than the style of cutting).

This characterization covers quite a range of market fish. To be precise, it describes fish of very low fat content (under 2 percent fat) with a taste that can be described as mild (not muddy, oily, rich — your fishman can give you good clues here). These fish also look lean, lacking the oily sheen of salmon or sablefish (also called butterfish). When cooked, the flesh becomes firm and flakes easily. For choices you can make, see the information at right headed "Interchangeable Fish."

Also getting some detailed attention in this chapter are conservative ways with squid for the adventurous, and adventurous treatments of tuna for the conservative — the one being so inexpensive and the other such a staple.

Greenland Turbot Salad with Louis Dressing

This salad resembles the West Coast classic, Crab Louis. But inexpensive Greenland turbot is used instead of the Dungeness crab, as it is remarkably similar in texture. Any other mild, firm, white-fleshed fish is good in the salad, too.

    2 cups water
    3 lemon slices
    1 *each* medium-size onion and carrot,
        thickly sliced
    1 teaspoon salt
   ¼ teaspoon pepper
    1 stalk celery
      About 2 pounds thawed Greenland turbot
        fillets, about ½ inch thick (or see
        Interchangeable Fish, below)
   ⅓ cup finely chopped sweet pickles
  1½ cups thinly sliced celery
      Louis dressing (recipe follows)
      Romaine or iceberg lettuce
    3 hard-cooked eggs, peeled and quartered
      Cherry tomatoes

In a large frying pan combine water, lemon, onion, carrot, salt, pepper, and celery; bring to a boil and then simmer for 10 minutes. Push vegetables to one side, set fish in pan, and spoon some of the vegetables over the fish. Return to a boil, cover, and simmer for 6 to 10 minutes or until thickest portions of fish flake readily when prodded with a fork. Remove from heat and chill fish in cooking liquid. Drain fish, discarding liquid, vegetables, and lemon. Pat fish dry and break into bite-size pieces.

Gently blend fish, pickles, sliced celery, and about ¾ cup of the dressing. Line a serving platter or individual plates with lettuce and mound salad on top. Garnish with eggs and cherry tomatoes.

Pass remaining dressing in a bowl at the table. Makes 4 to 6 servings.

Louis dressing. Mix ½ cup *each* mayonnaise and sour cream with ⅓ cup tomato-based chile sauce, 1 tablespoon lemon juice, and 3 tablespoons chopped green onion (with some tops); stir until blended.

Interchangeable Fish

A variety of mild, firm, white-fleshed fish can be used interchangeably in the following recipes.

Here are the names of the fish you can buy (depending on where you live); choose the one that has the best price: giant sea bass (also called black sea bass, grouper bass, sea bass), grouper, white sea bass, totuava, Pacific cod (also called true cod, gray cod, sea bass), redfish or drum (also called red drum, black drum), jumping mullet (also called black mullet), rockfish (also called rock cod, sea bass, rosefish, grouper, red snapper, Pacific ocean perch, and many more names), sole (also called petrale, rex, sand dab, flounder, turbot, and more), turbot, Greenland turbot, snapper (also called red snapper), sea trout, lingcod, halibut, haddock, and certain small shark.

As you can see, not only are the fish interchangeable, but at market level, the names are often applied to more than one fish.

Fish and Chips

The secret of presenting fish and chips is to be completely organized. Then serve this English favorite piping hot. (Consider the wok, page 23, for this job.)

    2 to 2½ pounds of mild, firm, white-fleshed
        fish fillets, *each* ½ to ¾ inch thick (see
        Interchangeable Fish, at left)
  1½ pounds frozen French-fried potatoes
      Salad oil
    1 cup all-purpose flour, unsifted
   ½ teaspoon paprika
   ¼ teaspoon salt
   ⅛ teaspoon pepper
   ¾ cup beer
      Malt vinegar
      Salt
      Lemon wedges

If fish is frozen, thaw completely, rinse, and pat dry. Cut fillets into 3 by 5-inch chunks.

Start by frying potatoes: heat 1½ to 2 inches salad oil in a deep pan and fry potatoes as directed on package; drain on absorbent material; put in a warm oven.

Combine flour, paprika, salt, pepper, and beer and beat until smooth.

To cook fish: bring salad oil to 375° on a deep-fat-frying thermometer. Dip each piece of fish in batter, drain briefly, then put into hot fat; cook a few pieces at a time, turning, until golden brown (3 to 4 minutes). Remove with a slotted spoon, drain briefly, and put in oven with potatoes until all are fried.

Serve with malt vinegar, salt, and lemon wedges to sprinkle onto each portion. Makes 4 to 6 servings.

Braised Fish Portuguese

Any firm, mild, white-fleshed fish described in the beginning of this chapter will go well with this mild tomato sauce.

    1 large onion, sliced
    3 tablespoons olive oil or salad oil
    ½ bay leaf
    1 clove garlic, minced or pressed
    1 large can (1 lb. 12 oz.) pear-shaped
        tomatoes
    1 tablespoon chopped parsley
    1 cup dry white wine (or ¼ cup lemon
        juice with ¾ cup water)
    1 teaspoon salt
    2 to 2½ pounds lingcod steaks or fillets, about
        ½ to ¾ inch thick (or see Interchangeable
        Fish, page 59)
      Chopped parsley
      Lemon wedges

In a 12-inch frying pan, saute onion in oil until soft. Add bay, garlic, tomatoes and juice, parsley, wine, and salt. Simmer, uncovered, stirring occasionally and breaking up tomatoes, for about 15 minutes. Set fish into sauce, not overlapping pieces. Simmer slowly, uncovered (spoon sauce over fish several times), until fish flakes when tested with a fork (about 12 to 15 minutes, depending on size of pieces). Transfer fish to a serving plate and keep warm. Boil sauce rapidly until reduced enough to thicken slightly; pour over fish. Sprinkle with parsley. Pass lemon wedges to squeeze over fish to taste. Makes about 6 servings.

Oven-fried Halibut

Other fish steaks listed in Interchangeable Fish (page 59), as well as swordfish or shark, can be cooked this way.

    About 2 pounds halibut steaks, cut 1
        inch thick
    2 to 3 tablespoons butter or margarine
      Salt
      About ¼ cup *each* yellow cornmeal and
        all-purpose flour

Choose a shallow baking pan in which fish will fit easily without crowding. Place butter in pan and melt in a 500° oven. Sprinkle fish with salt. Blend cornmeal and flour and coat fish evenly with it. Turn fish over in melted butter and arrange in baking pan.

Bake in the 500° oven for 8 to 12 minutes or until fish flakes easily when prodded in the thickest part with a fork or knife tip. Turn fish over after the first 5 minutes. Makes 5 or 6 servings.

How Long to Cook a Fish

What does it mean to "cook until fish flakes"? When cooked, the fibers that hold the fish together break down, and when the flesh is pushed or pulled, as with a fork, it comes apart easily or slides apart along the fine natural divisions you can see. Testing should be done in the thickest part of the fish, right against any bone. You will also notice a different look—cooked sections are opaque; uncooked sections have a translucent quality.

Curry-broiled Fish Fillets

Fillets or flat pieces of halibut, flounder, swordfish, shark, lingcod, or rockfish are all good cooked this easy way.

    1½ cups fresh bread crumbs (whirl bread
            pieces in blender)
    ⅓ cup mayonnaise
    2 teaspoons curry powder
      About 1½ pounds fish fillets (see
        Interchangeable Fish, page 59), ½
        to ¾ inch thick, cut in serving pieces
      Salt
    2 tablespoons butter or margarine
    2 tablespoons finely chopped chutney or
        ginger marmalade
    2 tablespoons lime or lemon juice

Spread bread crumbs in a shallow pan; broil about 5 inches from heat, stirring often, until toasted; then set aside. Combine the mayonnaise with curry powder. Sprinkle fish lightly with salt.

Spread one side of each fillet with mayonnaise mixture, using half of it. Turn fillets, mayonnaise side down, in the crumbs; spread second sides with remaining mayonnaise and coat with remaining crumbs. Transfer fillets to a well-greased shallow baking pan. Place 5 inches below heat and broil for about 6 to 8 minutes, until fish flakes when tested with a fork; turn once with a wide spatula.

Meanwhile melt the butter in a small pan. Stir in the chutney and lime juice; set aside.

With spatula, transfer fillets to warm serving plate. Accompany with chutney butter. Makes 4 servings.

Baked Fish with Mushroom Sauce

Well in advance of serving time you oven-poach any of the fish suggested in Interchangeable Fish (page 59). The flavorful sauce, which masks the fish, includes the oven-poaching liquid; it is also made ahead. The completed dish bakes just long enough to heat through.

When artichokes are in season, they make a fine first course or accompaniment for the fish. Also serve a salad and perhaps a make-ahead dessert such as a fresh fruit tart.

  1½ to 2 pounds skinless fish fillets or steaks (see above), each no more than 1 inch thick; fold in half fillets that are less than ½ inch thick
      About ½ cup regular-strength chicken broth or dry white wine
  1 teaspoon lemon juice
      Salt
      Mushroom sauce (directions follow)
  ¾ cup shredded Swiss cheese
      Ground nutmeg

Arrange fish pieces side by side in a shallow, close-fitting casserole (size required varies with shape of fish). Pour broth or wine over fish; add lemon juice and sprinkle lightly with salt. Cover and bake in a 400° oven for 10 to 22 minutes (shorter time for thin pieces, maximum time for thick pieces) or until fish flakes easily when prodded in thickest portion. Let cool slightly.

Holding fish in place with a wide spatula or pan lid, drain juices into a measuring cup. Cover and chill fish.

You should have about 1 cup liquid, but this varies with the fish — either boil juices to reduce to 1 cup, or add wine or broth to make 1 cup. Reserve to use hot or cold in mushroom sauce.

Spoon cooled mushroom sauce evenly over cold cooked fish, covering completely. Scatter cheese over sauce. (You can cover and continue chilling until time to complete meal.)

Bake fish, uncovered, in a 400° oven for 10 to 12 minutes or until sauce around edges is bubbling and cheese has melted. Dust very lightly with nutmeg. Makes 3 to 5 servings.

Mushroom sauce. Cook ½ pound thinly sliced mushrooms in 2 tablespoons butter or margarine, stirring, until mushrooms are limp and juices have evaporated. Set mushrooms aside. Melt 2 more tablespoons butter or margarine in pan and blend in 3 tablespoons all-purpose flour. Remove from heat and gradually stir in the 1 cup liquid reserved from cooked fish (preceding), ½ cup half-and-half (light cream), and ⅛ teaspoon ground nutmeg. Bring to a boil, stirring, and cook 1 or 2 minutes until thickened. Remove from heat, add mushrooms, and salt to taste. Chill, covered, until ready to use.

Fresh Is Best

Because of its delicate physical make-up, fish doesn't have the storage life of meat and should be used as soon as possible after purchase. Try to use it the day you buy it, or keep it refrigerated and use it within 24 hours. If kept longer, fish can be frozen; however, see "Freezing Fish" (below).

Oven-steamed Fish

Accompany this fish with any seasoning you like at serving time, such as seasoned salt or herb blends, tartar sauce, mayonnaise, prepared horseradish, hollandaise. Or perhaps just a squeeze of lemon and a pat of butter is more to your taste.

  1 pound boneless fish fillets (see Interchangeable Fish, page 59), about ½-inch maximum thickness
      About 2 to 3 tablespoons water
      Salt

Place fish fillets side by side in a close fitting pan (if you use sole fillets, fold in half or stack two together for thickness). Add water (just enough to moisten pan bottom) and sprinkle lightly with salt. Cover pan tightly. Bake fish in a 400° oven, 12 to 14 minutes, or until it just flakes readily when prodded in the thickest portion with a fork.

Serve hot or cold; to chill, leave in pan and refrigerate at least 2 hours. Makes 2 or 3 servings.

Freezing Fish

If you plan to make a large purchase of specially priced fish for your freezer, be sure to learn whether or not it has been frozen (and request that it be kept frozen if it has); fish that is *refrozen* suffers loss of flavor quality and texture. Much fish taken commercially is frozen as it's caught, though it may be thawed for sale.

Newport Red Pepper Chowder

Sour cream gives a refreshing tang to this hearty supper soup. When red bell peppers are not in season, you can use green peppers in their place.

4 tablespoons butter, margarine, or
  salad oil
2 medium-size onions, chopped
½ pound mushrooms, sliced (optional)
1 tablespoon lemon juice
2 large red bell peppers, seeded and thinly
  sliced
2 cans (about 14 oz. *each*) or 3½ cups
  regular-strength chicken broth
1 pound new potatoes, peeled and sliced
2 tablespoons *each* cornstarch and water
1 cup sour cream
1½ to 2 pounds boneless skinned fish (see
  Interchangeable Fish, page 59)
½ cup minced parsley
  Salt and pepper
  Lemon wedges

Melt butter in a 4 to 5-quart kettle. Add onions, mushrooms, lemon juice, and peppers, and cook on medium-high heat, stirring, until vegetables are limp (about 5 minutes). Add broth and potatoes. Bring to a boil, cover, and simmer gently for about 15 minutes or until potatoes are tender to pierce.

Blend cornstarch and water smoothly. Stir into sour cream; then gradually add some of the soup liquid to cream. Stir cream into soup; bring to a boil, stirring gently. Cut fish in bite-size chunks and add fish and parsley to soup; return to a boil; then cover and simmer for about 5 minutes or until fish flakes.

Serve soup hot, or chill, then reheat slowly just until steaming. Season to taste with salt and pepper and accompany with lemon wedges. Makes 6 to 8 generous servings.

Barbecued Sablefish, Teriyaki

Sablefish, also sold fresh as butterfish or black cod, is a modestly priced common market fish with very white flesh. It is quite different, though, in character and flavor from the fishes used interchangeably in the preceding recipes, and it should not be considered as an alternate for any of them. Sablefish is higher in fat content (on a par with salmon) and has a very tender or soft, mild-tasting flesh.

A Cold Supper from Provence

Aioli: Cold Oven-steamed Fish (page 61)
Hard-cooked Eggs in Shells   Radishes
Green Peppers   Tomatoes
Green Onions
Aioli Sauce
French Bread   Butter
Strawberries with Lemon Juice and Sugar

In the south of France a peasant dish known as *aioli* (pronounced eye-*oh*-lee) consists of cooked and raw vegetables and fish served with a pungent garlic mayonnaise. It can be a masterful production of hot and cold foods or a simple light meal such as this one for 4 or 5 people.

All the elements of the aioli can be organized well ahead, then chilled until time to assemble as a handsome platter for serving. A loaf of crusty bread and butter complete the main course.

You might like to offer strawberries in this French way: squeeze the juice from about ¼ of a lemon over each serving bowl filled with ¾ to 1 cup whole or sliced berries; then sprinkle with sugar to taste.

Aioli. On a wide, flat platter or tray, group each of the following foods separately. Lift chilled oven-steamed fish from its baking pan with large spatulas to preserve its shape, and place on the platter.

On one side of the fish, group 4 to 6 cold hard-cooked eggs. Trim stems and leaves from 1 bunch (about 1 cup) radishes and add to platter. Seed 2 green peppers and cut in wide strips; slice 2 large tomatoes; trim root end from 8 to 10 green onions; place these foods on the platter, arranging attractively. If desired, sprinkle the fish with a little minced parsley. Accompany with the bowl of aioli sauce (directions follow) to serve with each of the foods. Makes 4 or 5 servings.

For aioli sauce, blend 1 cup mayonnaise with 2 teaspoons Dijon mustard and 1 teaspoon minced or pressed garlic. Cover and chill several hours to blend flavors.

2 to 3-pound section of sablefish
¼ cup soy sauce
½ cup dry Sherry or apple juice
2 tablespoons lemon juice
½ teaspoon grated fresh ginger root (or
    ¼ teaspoon ground ginger)

Cut fish lengthwise into 2 fillets, removing back bone. Cut pieces of heavy foil the same size as fillets and place one against skin side of each section of fish.

In a small pan combine soy, Sherry, lemon juice, and ginger. Bring to a full rolling boil. Brush some of this sauce on flesh sides of fish and let stand 30 minutes.

Set fish, foil side down, on a grill 6 inches above a solid, even bed of completely ignited charcoal briquets (about 1 layer deep). Cover with a loose tent of foil or a barbecue hood (with drafts wide open). Cook for about 15 minutes or until fish flakes when prodded in thickest portion. Brush frequently with sauce, using all. Makes 4 to 6 servings.

Smoked Sablefish

Though sablefish is most often seen in its fresh form, it is also available smoked. Unlike the fresh fish, the smoked sablefish has firm texture and robust flavor resembling kippered salmon, but it is considerably lower in cost. Smoked sablefish—or kippered cod, smoked Alaska cod (see following recipe), barbecued Alaska cod, or smoked black cod—is usually sealed by the chunk in plastic bags; you find it in the refrigerated case of your supermarket.

Hot Smoked Sablefish

Small, boiled new potatoes, hard-cooked eggs, an omelet, and a green vegetable such as broccoli are all interesting with smoked sablefish (see note on Smoked Sablefish, above). Serve fish with the simple cheese sauce or melted butter and lemon juice.

1½ pounds smoked sablefish (Alaska cod)
    Cheese sauce (recipe follows) or melted
        butter and lemon juice to taste

To warm and soften the sablefish on top of the range, place fish in the top of a double boiler over simmering water; cover and heat for about 20 minutes.

To warm in oven, place smoked sablefish in a pan, cover, and bake at 325° for about 20 minutes.

Serve with melted butter and lemon juice, or with cheese sauce.

Cheese sauce. Blend 1 small package (3 oz.) cream cheese with ¼ cup sour cream, ½ cup minced green onion (include some tops), ½ teaspoon *each* dry mustard and Worcestershire, and about 1 tablespoon milk to give sauce an easy-to-spoon consistency. Makes about 1 cup, or 6 servings.

Thawing Frozen Fish

Frozen fish loses less of its moisture and texture if thawed in the refrigerator. But if you need to thaw it quickly, immerse water-tight package of fish in cold running water until flexible, and use at once. Drain off liquid and pat fish dry.

Stuffed Squid

Unless you really know what squid tastes like, chances are you'll be pleasantly puzzled as to the identity of these snowy morsels. The squid bakes to fork tenderness in a richly flavored pasta sauce that you serve on spaghetti.

18 large fresh or frozen, thawed squid
2 cans (15 oz. *each*) marinara sauce
2 cans (8 oz. *each*) minced clams
1 bay leaf
¾ cup thinly sliced green onions (including
    some of the tops)
1 pound ricotta cheese
¼ cup fine dry bread crumbs
½ teaspoon oregano leaves, crumbled
1 tablespoon finely chopped parsley
¼ cup finely chopped celery
1 egg
    Salt
6 ounces sliced mozzarella cheese
    Hot cooked spaghetti

Clean squid according to directions in Seafood Discovery: Squid (page 64).

In a pan, mix marinara sauce and liquid from clams; set clams aside. Add bay leaf and ¼ cup of the onions to the sauce. Bring sauce to a boil, reduce heat, and boil gently, uncovered, until thickened (about 30 minutes); stir often.

In a bowl, mix ricotta, crumbs, oregano, parsley, celery, egg, clams, and remaining chopped onion. Blend well; season to taste with salt. Stuff squid hoods with cheese mixture, using a small spoon or your fingers. (Or, to speed the process, slit squid hoods lengthwise and mound filling down one side; fold other side over top to enclose filling.)

Arrange stuffed hoods in a shallow 3-quart baking dish and top with body-leg sections. Pour marinara sauce over squid. Bake, uncovered, in a 400° oven for 20 minutes. Lay mozzarella slices over squid and bake until cheese melts and bubbles (about 5 minutes longer). Serve squid and sauce over individual portions of hot cooked spaghetti. Makes about 6 servings.

Fried Squid

For novices, these lightly crusted fried morsels are an easy introduction to squid; loops cut from the hood look like small fried onion rings, and the legs swirl into intricate curlicues.

   1 to 2 pounds fresh or thawed, frozen squid
     Garlic salt
     Equal portions fine dry bread crumbs and
       all-purpose flour (about 1 cup total
       for 1 lb. squid)
     Salad oil for frying

Seafood Discovery: Squid

The startling appearance of squid, or inkfish, very likely contributes to its bargain price. But this shellfish (its shell, a transparent, slender, sword-shaped piece, is inside the squid hood) is exceptionally delicate in both flavor and texture when properly cooked—likened most to the California luxury shellfish, abalone.

Squid is sometimes available fresh in coastal markets, and it is increasingly available in 1 to 3-pound frozen units in supermarkets and fish markets.

Before you cook the squid in the ways suggested in this book, you must clean it, following these steps:

1. Holding squid under running water, pull off and discard the speckled membrane that covers the hood (also called mantle).

2. Separate the body from the hood by gently drawing apart.

3. Pull the sword or shell from inside the hood and discard. Squeeze out and discard contents of the hood, and rinse inside the hood.

4. Strip off and discard any membrane and other material that separates easily from the body (including the ink sac).

5. Pop out and discard parrotlike beak from between the legs.

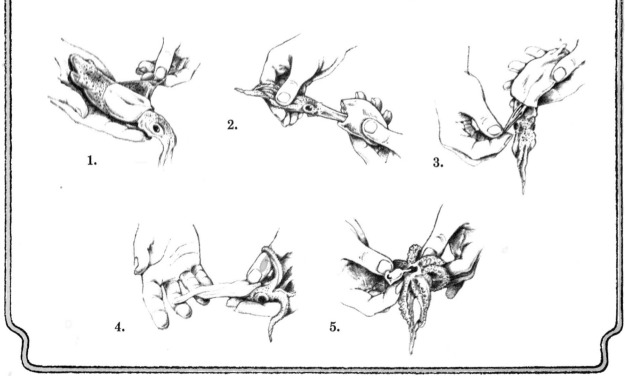

Clean squid as directed in Seafood Discovery: Squid (page 64).

Slice squid hoods crosswise in ¼ to ½-inch-wide strips (these are the rings). Drain squid rings and legs on absorbent material; then sprinkle with garlic salt. Coat squid with mixture of crumbs and flour; shake off excess.

In a deep pan (about 2-qt. size) or wok (page 23), heat 1½ inches salad oil to 375°. Cook rings a spoonful at a time for about 30 seconds or until lightly browned; if overcooked the squid gets rubbery.

Drain rings on absorbent material, keeping warm. Bring oil back to 375° before each addition. Cook body with legs last, also for about 30 seconds; as they tend to spatter, have a lid handy to cover pan loosely.

Serve squid hot. One pound of squid makes 2 or 3 servings.

Italian Tuna and Vegetable Pie

Traditional Italian seasonings flavor tuna and vegetables in this hearty main-dish pie. Accompany it with a green salad for a satisfying lunch or supper.

  1 can (14 oz.) tomato slices
  2 tablespoons olive oil or salad oil
  1 large onion, chopped
1½ cups thinly sliced carrot
  1 clove garlic, minced or pressed
  ½ cup tomato-based chile sauce
  1 teaspoon oregano leaves
  ⅛ teaspoon pepper
  2 tablespoons all-purpose flour
  1 can (2¼ oz.) sliced ripe olives, drained
  1 large can (12½ oz.) or 2 cans (6 or 7 oz. *each*) tuna, drained
1¼ cups freshly grated or shredded Parmesan cheese
    Pastry for a single-crust 9-inch pie (page 92)

Drain tomatoes thoroughly, saving juice; set aside.

Pour oil into a large frying pan over medium-high heat. Add onion, carrot, and garlic; cook, stirring, until carrot is tender. Add chile sauce, oregano, and pepper. Gradually blend reserved tomato juice into flour; pour into onion mixture. Cook, stirring, until thickened. Remove from heat and add olives, tuna, and ½ cup of the cheese; mix gently; set aside.

Roll out pastry to fit a 9-inch pie pan; flute edge and spoon in filling. Arrange tomatoes over top and sprinkle with remaining ¾ cup cheese.

Bake in a 375° oven for about 35 minutes or until crust is golden and pie is hot. Let stand about 10 minutes before serving. Makes 6 servings.

Minted Tuna Salad

Fresh mint and limes give a refreshing flavor to this whole-meal salad.

  ½ teaspoon grated lime peel
  3 tablespoons lime juice
  2 tablespoons chopped fresh mint or crumbled dried mint leaves
  2 cans (6 or 7 oz. *each*) tuna, drained
1½ cups cold cooked rice
  1 cup *each* thinly sliced celery and frozen peas, thawed
  2 tablespoons *each* chopped green onion and parsley
    Mustard dressing (recipe follows)
    Salt and pepper
    Crisp salad greens and mint sprigs

Combine lime peel and juice, mint, tuna, rice, celery, peas, onion, and parsley; stir gently to mix well. Cover and chill for at least 2 hours.

To serve, mix mustard dressing gently with tuna mixture. Season to taste with salt and pepper. Spoon into a lettuce-lined salad bowl and garnish with mint sprigs. Makes 6 servings.

Mustard dressing. Combine 1 teaspoon Dijon mustard, 2 teaspoons sugar, and ½ teaspoon liquid hot pepper seasoning. Gradually stir in ½ cup mayonnaise and ¼ cup buttermilk.

When the Fish Have Been Biting

When you have a quantity of fresh fish, you might freeze it in this manner:

Eviscerate the fish at once and scale if necessary. Cut in steaks, fillets, or other cooking-size pieces. If desired, leave head and tail on small fish.

Arrange pieces of fish on a baking sheet and freeze until solid; within a few hours, pop off pan (by flexing), slip pieces into freezer bags, and seal. This way you can use the fish in any quantity.

Meatless Entrees with Style

Chances are if you enjoy omelets, souffles, macaroni and cheese, cheese filled enchiladas, savory beans, lentil soup, and other dishes of this kind, you've already based many a meal upon them for the most important reason of all—they taste good. But when you're investigating means of economizing, these good protein source foods wave another flag—a price tag. Generally speaking, for equal nutrition per serving, they cost considerably less than meat and fish.

We don't advocate eliminating meat or fish from the diet. But for variety, freshness in meal planning, and holding the line on food costs, this chapter's meatless dishes and those lightly supplemented by meat are good main-dish choices.

The increasingly popular soybean, a most nutritious legume, is explored flavorfully, with a special focus on ways to cook with the soybean curd called *tofu*. For yogurt lovers, there is a bonus of directions for making your own, starting with ingredients you can keep on hand at all times.

Macaroni and Cheese Plus

The technique used in making this dish is about as direct as you can get. While the macaroni boils, heat any smoothly melting cheese along with a flavorful liquid, stirring until creamy. Then add the drained macaroni. To give a finished look, slip under the broiler for a minute or two to lightly brown the surface.

The beauty is the mix-and-match potential of the ingredients. Pick any shape noodle or macaroni (perhaps a vegetable-flavored pasta). Try a variety of cheeses such as any pasteurized processed cheese (including hickory smoked cheese and chile-flavored cheese) or other good natural melters like longhorn or mild Cheddar, teleme, jack, Samsoe, Havarti, Gruyere. Thin them as you like with milk, wine, beer, or broth.

    8 ounces macaroni or noodles
    3 to 4 quarts boiling water
      Salt
      About 2 teaspoons salad oil or melted butter
        or margarine
    ¾ pound cheese, shredded (suggestions
        precede)
    2 to 8 tablespoons milk, buttermilk, Sherry,
        beer, dry white wine, or regular-strength
        chicken or beef broth
      About 1 cup seasoned croutons (optional)

Pour macaroni into boiling salted water and let cook, uncovered, according to package directions.

Meanwhile, coat a wide frying pan with oil and cover with cheese. Set on low to medium-low heat; when cheese starts to melt, stir, adding a little liquid at a time to make consistency you want.

Drain cooked macaroni in a colander. When cheese is melted, stir in macaroni and salt to taste. If you like, sprinkle croutons over macaroni and cheese and then slip pan about 2 inches below heat source and broil 1 or 2 minutes or until lightly browned. Serve at once. Makes about 4 servings.

Cheese Enchiladas

Two kinds of cheese and chopped green onions make a substantial filling in these enchiladas. Serve them as the main course, with a platter of cold cooked vegetables such as turnips, zucchini, green beans, or green and red peppers drenched with an oil and vinegar dressing.

You can assemble the enchiladas hours ahead and then bake to serve.

      Salad oil
    1 package (12) corn tortillas
    1 can (7 oz.) green chile salsa
      Cheese filling (directions follow)
    2 cups shredded longhorn or Cheddar cheese
      About 1 cup finely shredded iceberg lettuce
    2 medium-size tomatoes, thinly sliced
      About ¼ cup thinly sliced green onions
        (including some tops)
    1 tablespoon vinegar
      Salt

In a small frying pan heat about ¼ inch salad oil over moderate heat. Fry one tortilla at a time, turning once, just until limp but not crisp; drain on absorbent material. Add oil to pan as needed.

Pour about ⅓ of the green chile salsa into a shallow 9 by 12-inch casserole or pan (or one with equivalent area). Place two tortillas side by side, overlapping, to fill width of pan. Let them drape partially over end of pan. Spoon about ⅔ cup filling onto overlapped tortillas across width of pan, and fold draped ends over filling, to form first set of enchiladas. Repeat this procedure to fill remaining tortillas; let each pair of tortillas overlap the pair before.

Tuck ends under last set of enchiladas. Moisten surface of enchiladas with remaining green chile salsa and cover with shredded cheese. At this point you can cover and chill the dish.

Bake, uncovered, in a 375° oven for 20 minutes (if chilled, bake 30 minutes, covered for the first 15 minutes) or until bubbling. Garnish enchiladas with lettuce, tomatoes, and green onions. Sprinkle vinegar and salt over vegetables. Makes 6 servings.

Cheese filling. Stir together to blend 1½ pints (3 cups) large curd cottage cheese, 1 cup shredded longhorn or Cheddar cheese, 1½ cups finely chopped green onions (including some of the tops), and ¼ teaspoon oregano leaves, crumbled.

Cheese: from the Freezer and Refrigerator

Maximum recommended freezer storage time for well-wrapped natural cheeses is about 8 weeks; pasteurized processed cheeses can be frozen about twice as long. You may find some cheeses like Parmesan, Cheddar, jack, or cream cheese are inclined to crumble after thawing; they are still fine for use in cooking. Richer, creamy cheeses like Camembert and Brie freeze with little apparent loss in quality.

Cheese that has become moldy, even when stored in the refrigerator, should be well trimmed of all the mold; then if the cheese has a fresh aroma (not soured), go ahead and serve it.

Cherry Cheese Blintzes

Golden on the outside, creamy on the inside characterizes these intriguing Russian-Jewish blintzes. The cheese filling is flavored by onions cooked mellow, sweet, and amber; the topping is hot cherry sauce and cold sour cream. Surprisingly, the sweetness of the vegetable and the fruit meld deliciously.

As an entree for supper or lunch, blintzes go well before or after soup or salad. You can shape the blintzes well ahead, but they should be sauteed just before serving.

    Cheese filling (directions follow)
20 to 24 crepes (page 37—use 1½ times the
        recipe; if preparing specifically for this
        dish, cook *each crepe on one side only*)
    About 6 tablespoons *each* salad oil and
        butter or margarine
    Sour cream
    Sweet cherry sauce (directions follow)

To make each blintz, make a rectangular mound of about 3 tablespoons of cheese filling in the center of the browned side of each crepe. Enclose the filling by folding opposite sides of the crepe up and over the filling to make a rectangular bundle; set seam side down.

In a wide frying pan over high heat, melt 3 tablespoons butter in about 3 tablespoons salad oil. Place blintzes seam side down in pan, without crowding. Fry until golden brown on each side (about 2 minutes total). Transfer to a platter and keep warm until all are cooked. Add more butter and oil to pan as needed.

Spoon sour cream onto each serving of blintzes and top with sweet cherry sauce. Makes 20 to 24 blintzes (6 or 7 servings).

Cheese filling. Finely chop 1 large onion and cook in 2 tablespoons melted butter or margarine in a frying pan over medium heat for about 20 minutes until golden brown, stirring frequently. Beat cooked onions and butter, 1 large package (8 oz.) cream cheese, and 1½ pounds pot cheese (also called farmer's cheese) until smoothly blended.

Or instead of pot cheese you can use 2 pints (4 cups) large curd cottage cheese, dried as follows: spread on a muslin cloth (such as a tea towel) and then wrap up in the towel, twisting to wring out as much moisture as possible; unwrap and scrape cheese from cloth. Makes about 4 cups filling.

Sweet cherry sauce. Pit 2 to 3 cups sweet cherries (Bing, if available, or use drained canned pitted sweet cherries). In a pan combine 2 teaspoons cornstarch, ¼ cup sugar, ½ cup water (or use ½

cup canned sweet cherry juice instead of water and sugar), and 2 teaspoons lemon juice. Bring to a boil rapidly, stirring, until sauce is thickened. Use hot or set aside and reheat to simmering at serving time.

Spinach Crepes

Broiled tomatoes and mushrooms are an attractive side dish for these cheese rich, main-dish crepes. You can freeze the filled crepes, heating a few at a time to serve.

 3 tablespoons butter or margarine
 1 large onion, thinly sliced
 2 pounds spinach
⅔ cup whipping cream
½ teaspoon lemon juice
    Salt
12 to 16 crepes (page 37)
 3 cups (about ¾ lb.) shredded Swiss cheese
    Sour cream

Melt butter in a 4 to 5-quart kettle. Add onion and cook over medium heat, stirring occasionally, until limp and pale gold (about 20 minutes).

Meanwhile discard stems and yellowed leaves from spinach and wash green spinach leaves well in several changes of water. Drain; then chop spinach coarsely and add to onions. Cover and cook until leaves are limp (about 2 to 3 minutes). Stir in cream and lemon juice and cook over high heat, stirring, until most of the liquid evaporates; salt to taste.

Divide filling and 2 cups of the cheese equally among the crepes, spooning both down the center of each crepe; roll to enclose.

(If made ahead, freeze filled crepes, seam side down and slightly apart, on a baking sheet, uncovered. When crepes are firmly frozen, pop free by flexing pan and then package them airtight.)

To heat and serve, arrange desired number of freshly made or frozen crepes, side by side, seams down, in a shallow casserole or individual rame-kins. Cover and bake in a 375° oven for 20 minutes (35 to 40 minutes, if frozen). Uncover and sprinkle evenly with remaining cheese (allowing 1 to 1½ tablespoons per crepe) and return to oven until cheese melts (about 5 minutes). Accompany with sour cream. Allow 3 to 4 crepes for a serving; makes 4 to 6 servings.

Quiche Lorraine

The traditional quiche Lorraine is a delicate cheese custard flavored with bacon. It makes an elegantly simple supper entree.

10 slices cooked bacon, coarsely chopped
1¼ cups (about 6 oz.) diced or thinly sliced Swiss cheese
     9 or 10-inch baked pastry shell (page 92)
 4 eggs
1¼ cups whipping cream
 ½ cup milk
     Freshly grated nutmeg or ground nutmeg

Evenly distribute bacon and cheese over bottom of pastry shell. Beat eggs until they are blended; then mix well with cream and milk. Pour liquid over cheese and bacon; grate nutmeg over filling.

Bake in a 325° oven for about 40 minutes or until custard appears firm when dish is gently shaken (it may puff slightly, too). Let stand 10 minutes; cut in wedges. Makes 6 to 8 servings.

Raclette—A Simple Peasant Meal

Green Salad or Vegetable Soup
Raclette
Hot Boiled or Baked Potatoes
Marinated Onions and Sweet Pickles
Poached Apples with Cream

The ultimate in simplicity is the Swiss peasant meal, *raclette*. A chunk of cheese is placed by the heat—at the fireplace or under the broiler—until it softens and begins to melt. Then you scrape off the melted cheese, spoon it over bites of hot boiled or baked potato, and eat with zesty marinated onion or sweet pickle. Wine, green salad or vegetable soup, and a light dessert, such as poached apples or pears make a complete fireside menu (if you don't have a fireplace, serve the broiled cheese in individual portions at the table).

Prepare onion mixture and allow to marinate while potatoes are baking. When potatoes are done, pour onions into one serving bowl, pickles into another, and pass hot potatoes on individual serving plates to your guests.

2 to 3 pounds (preferably one chunk) of one of the following cheeses: raclette, jack, fontina, Gruyere, Samsoe, or Swiss
   Boiled or baked potatoes (directions follow)
   Marinated onions (recipe follows)
2 cups small sweet pickles

To prepare and serve raclette at the fire-place, place cheese, trimmed of any wax, in a shallow rimmed pan. Make just one portion of raclette (or what you plan to eat at once) at a time. Set pan on hearth and push wide surface of cheese close to fire. When cheese face begins to melt, scrape it off, spoon onto a bite of hot potato, and eat with marinated onions and sweet pickles.

Pull cheese away from heat until you are ready for next serving; each person can tend to his or her own needs, helping him or herself to onions, pickles, and cheese.

If you are without a fireplace, you can broil the cheese. Arrange ½-inch-thick slices, side by side, to cover the bottom of a shallow pan (such as a pie pan). Broil about 4 inches from heat until melted and bubbling; serve at once. Have as many pans of cheese as you will need; broil when ready to serve. Makes 6 to 8 servings.

Boiled or baked potatoes. Scrub 3 pounds very small new potatoes and boil in water to cover until tender when pierced (about 20 minutes). Drain off most of the water and set potatoes, covered, next to fire to keep warm during meal.

Or select 6 to 8 medium-size baking potatoes. Wash, dry, pierce each potato in one or two places with a sharp fork, and place on rack in a 400° oven. Bake about 1 hour until potatoes give easily when pressed. Slit top of each potato in an X and then press sides to force some of the white of the potato to the surface. Spoon hot cheese into center to eat.

Marinated onions. Thinly slice 2 medium-size white or red onions. Mix with ⅓ cup white wine vinegar, ½ teaspoon salt, and 1½ teaspoons sugar. Cover and let chill at least 1 hour; mix occasionally. Makes 6 servings.

Cheese, Onion, and Chile Pie

A California twist of the quiche—chiles, onions, and cheese in a pie. A cooked sauce is the base, giving the pie a firmer texture than the quiche Lorraine. Accompany with an avocado and tomato salad.

        3 tablespoons butter or margarine
        2 large onions, thinly sliced
        4 tablespoons all-purpose flour
        1 cup milk
        3 eggs, beaten
     1/4 teaspoon salt
        1 large can (7 oz.) California green chiles,
            seeded and chopped
        1 cup shredded longhorn or mild Cheddar
            cheese
        1 cup jack cheese
        1 baked 9-inch pastry shell (page 92)

In a wide frying pan, melt butter over medium heat. Add onions and cook, stirring, until onions are limp and begin to brown slightly (about 15 to 20 minutes). Stir in flour. Remove from heat and gradually blend in milk. Return to heat and bring to a boil, stirring; cook until thickened. Let cool about 5 minutes; then gradually stir in eggs, salt, chiles, and cheese. Pour into pastry shell and bake in a 325° oven for about 40 minutes or until filling is firm when pan is gently shaken.

Let stand at least 10 minutes to cool slightly before cutting in wedges to serve. Makes 6 servings.

Chiles Rellenos Casserole

Instead of frying these cheese stuffed chiles, as is typical, you bake them in a puffy egg batter. The casserole is served with a canned sauce. To complete the menu, have crisp radishes, a mixed bean salad, and for dessert, poached or canned plums with sour cream. A colorful meal, it is quick and easy to assemble.

        1 can (4 oz.) California green chiles
     1/4 to 1/3 pound jack cheese
        4 eggs
     1/3 cup milk
     1/2 cup all-purpose flour, unsifted
     1/2 teaspoon baking powder
        1 cup shredded sharp Cheddar cheese
        1 can (15 oz.) marinara sauce
            Pitted ripe olives

Remove seeds and pith from chiles. Cut jack cheese in large chunks and divide evenly among chiles, folding or tucking cheese inside. Butter a medium-depth 1 1/2-quart casserole and arrange chiles in it, side by side.

With a wire whisk or electric mixer, beat eggs until thick and foamy; then add milk, flour, and baking powder; beat until smooth. Pour egg batter over chiles, moistening evenly the surface of all chiles. Sprinkle with Cheddar cheese. Bake, uncovered, in a 375° oven for about 30 minutes or until casserole is puffed and appears set when gently shaken.

Just before casserole is ready, heat marinara sauce to simmering.

Garnish hot casserole quickly with pitted ripe olives and serve at once. Pass marinara sauce to spoon over. Makes 4 servings.

Huevos Rancheros

Huevos rancheros, or Mexican country-style eggs, are more than just a dish—properly served they become a meal. The eggs (fried, or sometimes poached or scrambled) are served atop mildly sauced, lightly fried tortillas garnished with buttery avocado and invariably accompanied by refried beans (you can dress up canned beans or serve the ones on page 76).

Because there are several parts to this dish, it is easier to prepare the sauce and fry the tortillas ahead; you reheat these ingredients while the refried beans bake, and then fry the eggs and assemble.

        2 medium-size onions, finely chopped
        1 tablespoon salad oil
        1 can (10 oz.) red chile sauce
        1 can (8 oz.) tomato sauce
     1/2 teaspoon oregano leaves
        1 tablespoon butter or margarine
        1 can (1 lb.) refried beans
     1/2 cup shredded jack or Cheddar cheese
        6 hot fried tortillas (directions follow)
        6 or 12 fried eggs (directions follow)
        2 medium-size avocados, peeled and sliced
            Prepared salsa jalapena

Cook onion in salad oil until soft; add chile sauce, tomato sauce, and oregano. Bring to a full boil; then simmer gently, uncovered, for 15 minutes; stir occasionally. Use hot, or cool and reheat.

Cut butter in small pieces and mix with refried beans; then spread beans in a small shallow casserole and sprinkle with cheese. Bake, uncovered, in a 350° oven for 15 minutes.

Dip each hot fried tortilla in heated sauce, coating both sides; then place tortillas on individual dishes or side by side on a large tray. Spoon all the sauce evenly over tortillas and top each with 1 or 2 hot fried eggs. Garnish with avocado slices. Pass salsa jalapena to be added as desired. Accompany with hot refried beans. Makes 6 servings.

Fried tortillas. Heat about ½ inch salad oil in a small frying pan over moderate heat. Fry corn tortillas, one at a time, until slightly crisp; turn frequently. Drain on absorbent material. Keep warm if you plan to serve at once, or let cool and then spread in a single layer on a baking sheet and bake at 350° for about 4 minutes.

Fried eggs. Melt 2 tablespoons butter or margarine in wide frying pan (use 2 pans for 12 eggs, or cook in succession). Break eggs into pan. Sprinkle with about ¼ cup shredded jack cheese and 1 tablespoon water. Cover and cook until eggs are set the way you like; salt to taste and transfer with a wide spatula onto sauce-coated tortillas.

Basic Omelet

Firm and golden outside, creamy and smooth inside, plain or filled—such an omelet is a tour-de-force for any cook. Once you've mastered the quick, direct technique, you'll count omelets among the showiest and most usable entrees in your repertoire.

You need an omelet pan and the confidence and necessary speed that come with a little practice. Then consider making omelets before your family or guests—in the kitchen or from an electric hot-plate at the table—turning out omelets one right after the other until all are served. It's not hard to become sufficiently skilled to cook two omelets at the same time.

Have a big green salad and bread and butter ready to serve before you start cooking. For a classically simple way to end your meal, serve fruit and cheese.

    1 tablespoon butter or margarine
    2 or 3 eggs
    2 or 3 teaspoons water
      About ⅛ teaspoon salt
    2 teaspoons seasoning (optional, suggestions
        follow)
    2 tablespoons filling (optional, suggestions
        follow)

You will need a 7 to 8-inch omelet pan with flared rim. Set pan on high heat with butter to melt while you quickly break eggs into a bowl. Add water (1 teaspoon per egg) and salt to bowl; beat with a fork just until whites and yolks are blended. (If you do several omelets, you can beat all the eggs together and then pour a portion at a time into omelet pan—to know how much to add, note depth of egg in pan when doing a single omelet.)

When butter is melted and just beginning to brown lightly and give off a nutty aroma, stir seasoning into butter, if desired, and then pour in eggs all at once. As soon as egg begins to turn opaque on the bottom (almost immediately), push cooked egg from the side and bottom of pan to well past the center, working quickly all around pan; this lets uncooked egg flow to pan bottom. Keep pushing cooked egg out of the way of uncooked, and shake pan occasionally to make sure omelet is free and not sticking. You do not want omelet to brown—browning makes eggs tough. When there is no more free-flowing liquid yet top still looks moist and creamy, quickly spoon filling across center of omelet, in line with pan handle. Holding pan in your left hand, and tilting it up to the right, quickly fold one side of the omelet half over the center. Then tilt pan over serving dish and gently shake unfolded side of omelet onto plate; quickly flip pan so that the omelet rolls out onto itself. The finished omelet will come to rest with both sides folded under it.

Serve omelet immediately; it continues to cook even as you hand the plate to a guest. (Or you can set the plate with omelet in a warm oven for as long as 5 minutes if you want to serve several people all at once.)

If a bit of egg sticks to your pan (as most often happens if you let the eggs brown), pour some salt in pan and rub free with a paper towel. Wipe pan clean and return to heat.

Makes 1 omelet (1 serving).

Seasoning. Minced parsley, chopped green onions, minced shallots, chopped tarragon or basil (or use ¼ teaspoon dried tarragon or dried basil).

Filling. Shredded Cheddar, Parmesan, Romano, Swiss, or jack cheese; sauteed mushroom slices; chopped canned California green chiles; chopped green pepper.

Egg Buying

Eggs are sold in six different sizes, according to weight per dozen and the uniformity of each egg's shape.

The minimum weight of a dozen jumbo eggs is 30 ounces; of extra large, 27 ounces; large, 24 ounces; medium, 21 ounces; small, 18 ounces; and pee wee, 14 ounces.

If the difference between the cost of one egg size and the next biggest size is less than 7 cents, you get more for your money if you buy the larger ones. Recipes in this book are tested with large eggs, but size is important only when the volume of the eggs is critical—such as when baking. To adjust for volume, keep in mind that 1 large egg measures about 3 tablespoons. For omelets, hard-cooked eggs, frying, or poaching, any size you like will be fine.

Spanish Omelet Picnic Loaf

Nestled inside a big, round loaf of French bread is a thick and hearty Spanish-style omelet made with onions, bell peppers, and chunks of potato, accented with flavorful bits of sausage. It is ideal for picnics, as you eat it out of hand.

The loaf, to many minds, improves with standing—the juices and flavors of the omelet permeate the bread. You can make it and keep it warm up to 4 hours; you can even make it a day ahead, chill; then reheat.

    1 large, round sourdough French loaf (about
        10 to 12 inches in diameter)
      About 4 tablespoons olive oil or salad oil
      About 10 ounces chorizo or linguisa sausage
    1 large new potato, cooked
    1 medium-size onion, finely chopped
    1 clove garlic, minced or pressed
    1 medium-size green pepper, seeded and
        chopped
    1 medium-size red bell pepper, seeded and
        chopped (or use 2 green peppers, total)
    9 eggs
   ¾ teaspoon salt
   ¼ teaspoon pepper

With a long serrated knife, split bread in half horizontally. Hollow out center of loaf, leaving a 1-inch-thick wall. Brush interior with about 1 tablespoon oil. Reassemble loaf and place in a 300° oven while preparing omelet.

In a 10-inch omelet pan or frying pan, crumble or cut up sausage, discarding casing. Saute until lightly browned. Remove sausage with slotted spoon and drain; discard drippings. Peel and thinly slice potato. Heat 1 tablespoon oil in pan over medium-high heat and add potato, onion, and garlic; cook, turning often, until nicely browned (about 3 minutes). Add green and red peppers and cook for 1 minute longer; stir in sausage and remove from heat.

With a fork, beat eggs until blended with salt and pepper. Return omelet pan to medium heat, push potato mixture to one side, and drizzle another 1 tablespoon oil over pan bottom. Spread vegetables out in pan and pour in eggs. As edges begin to set, push toward center with a wide spatula and shake pan vigorously to allow uncooked egg to flow underneath.

Cook omelet until top is just set but appears moist, and bottom is lightly browned (takes about 5 minutes). To turn omelet, run a wide spatula around edge and under to be sure it is free. Invert a plate or pan over omelet, and with one hand on the plate, the other gripping pan handle, quickly invert pan, turning omelet out onto the plate. Scrape any stuck bits free with spatula. Add remaining oil to pan, return to medium heat, and gently slide omelet back into pan. Cook until lightly browned on second side (about 2 minutes); remove from heat.

Remove bread from oven and separate halves. Invert bottom half of loaf over top of omelet; then quickly invert pan, turning omelet out into loaf. Set top of bread in place. Serve loaf hot. Or to keep warm up to 4 hours, wrap in a towel and several thicknesses of newspaper.

If made ahead, chill loaf and, when cold, wrap airtight. To reheat, wrap in foil and place in a 400° oven for about 25 to 30 minutes or until omelet is hot and steamy.

Cut in wedges. Makes about 6 servings.

Keep Cool

Waste not, stay well, and eat better. Follow the practice of promptly refrigerating protein foods—eggs, cheese, meat, poultry, fish—both fresh from the market and in the form of leftovers. Letting these foods stand at room temperature (60° to 120° is rated as the danger zone) considerably reduces their quality and gives bacteria a chance to grow.

Eggs, for example, deteriorate as quickly in 1 day at room temperature as they do in 1 week in the refrigerator.

Cheese Souffle

Try different cheeses, separately or in combinations, and different seasonings to vary this classic souffle. Taste the sauce to decide what to add.

3 tablespoons butter or margarine
3 tablespoons all-purpose flour
1 cup milk
Dash cayenne
¼ teaspoon dry mustard
½ teaspoon salt
1 cup shredded Cheddar cheese (mild to sharp) or Swiss cheese
4 or 5 eggs, separated

In a pan melt butter and stir in flour. Blend in milk, cayenne, dry mustard, and salt; cook, stirring, until thickened. Add cheese and continue stirring until melted. Remove from heat and beat in egg yolks.

Whip whites until they hold short, distinct peaks. Fold about half the whites thoroughly into sauce; fold in remaining whites as thoroughly as you like. Pour into well-buttered 1½-quart souffle dish (or 4 to 6 dishes of 1-cup size). Lightly etch a circle on surface of souffle, an inch or so in from rim, with tip of knife or spoon (this cut helps form the classic topknot shape of the crust).

Bake souffle in a 375° oven; a 1½-quart souffle takes 35 minutes; individual 1-cup souffles take 20 minutes. Makes 4 servings.

Making Your Own Yogurt

Yogurt making is a self-perpetuating process. You initially need a starter (or culture) of commercial or homemade yogurt to combine with milk. But once your first batch is made, some of it becomes the starter for your next yogurt, and on it goes.

There are many ways to make yogurt, usually with fresh milk. But this exceptionally fresh-tasting version uses milk products you can keep on hand at all times: canned evaporated milk and nonfat dry milk. You mix the milks with warm water and then add the starter, which grows and converts the thin liquid to a thick, tangy yogurt. The only trick is keeping the mixture at the right temperature for about 6 hours. If too cold, the starter doesn't work; if too warm, it dies.

In desert countries, where yogurt is a diet staple, the climate cooperates in its making. Here, electric yogurt makers are available, but you can achieve very accurate control with either a gas or electric range.

The first step is to test your heating system to learn how to control the temperature. To do this—and to make yogurt—you will need a large kettle with a rack (such as a canning kettle), an extra wire rack, a thermometer, and enough jars or glasses (of the same height) to hold about 2½ quarts.

Fill kettle with water up to the height of the jars (do not have jars in kettle). Heat water to 115°; then place on an electric cooking element or in a gas oven (with pilot) and manipulate according to following instructions until you can keep the water within a temperature range of 110° to 115° for 1 hour. (Under 90° the starter is inactive; over 120° it dies.) Once you figure out the routine, you can duplicate it as needed.

For an electric range. Set water-filled kettle on electric element at lowest heat setting. If temperature goes above 115°, use a wire rack to elevate kettle slightly. If temperature still goes too high, set jar rings (or cans—like those for tuna, with both ends removed) on rack to lift pan—keeping it steady—farther from heat.

For a gas range. Remove oven racks, set water-filled kettle directly over open pilot light (oven turned off), and close door. If temperature goes above 115°, raise kettle by setting on a wire rack (or to go higher, replace oven rack in lowest position). If pilot light does not give enough heat and oven has a 140° or low setting, place kettle on oven rack, turn oven on, and test until it holds proper temperature; open or close door or turn oven on and off to regulate.

The yogurt. In a pan combine 1 can (13 oz.) evaporated milk, 5 cups hot tap water, and 3 envelopes (or enough for 3 qt. milk) nonfat dry milk. Heat or cool mixture to 115°; then mix in ½ cup unflavored yogurt (commercial or homemade) and stir until well blended. Pour into clean jars (of same height), leaving about ¾ inch between liquid and rim; put on lids or cover with foil or clear plastic wrap. Set jars on rack in kettle (see preceding). Pour 115° water into kettle until it comes up to the level of liquid in jars. Maintain temperature of water between 110° and 115° according to instructions (see preceding), and check occasionally to be certain all is going well. Jars of liquid should not be disturbed for 5 to 6 hours or until yogurt is set and has consistency of soft custard. (There may be some liquid floating on top, but most will be absorbed during chilling.) Store covered yogurt in refrigerator. Makes 2 quarts.

The Secret of a Souffle

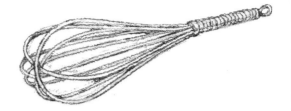

For showmanship, there's nothing like that fleeting moment when a souffle emerges from the oven, standing high, golden, and handsome in its dish. Contrary to rumor, it's not difficult to achieve the souffle's mystical airiness once you understand the basics.

Despite its seeming fragility, a souffle is hearty enough to make a whole meal when served with just salad, bread, and perhaps another vegetable—the essence of elegance, despite its intrinsic economy.

Simply stated, a souffle is a thick, flavored sauce, blended with egg yolks, folded together with whipped egg whites, and baked. Heat causes the many bubbles of air and moisture captured in the egg whites to expand, and the souffle rises grandly to a fragile golden brown creation whose surface usually cracks in several places to reveal the delicate, slightly moist interior. Within a few seconds after the souffle comes from the oven, the air inside begins to cool and contract and the souffle begins to fall.

Understanding the nature of a souffle opens doors for exploration in flavors.

The sauce must be the consistency of a thick white sauce (3 to 4 tablespoons all-purpose flour for each 1 cup liquid). This is perhaps the most important factor for success. If the sauce is too thin, the souffle may fall before it is cooked; if too thick, the sauce doesn't fold into the whites well and the souffle has less volume.

The egg whites should be whipped just to the point at which they hold short, distinct, moist-looking peaks—the tiny bubbles are still elastic enough to swell generously when the air inside heats and expands. Overbeating causes the finished souffle to have poor volume and taste dry; underbeating prevents it from rising as high as it might. Egg whites can be whipped with a hand whip, rotary beater, or electric beater.

The number of eggs in ratio to sauce can be varied to a surprising degree. One cup of thick sauce provides adequate support for four to nine eggs. Most of the following recipes call for whites and yolks equally, but you can change proportions if you have extras of either. One extra white for every four whole eggs, or one extra yolk for every three whole eggs won't alter the quality.

Extra yolks do give a souffle greater stability, though. The souffle proportionately rises higher, falls more slowly, and has slightly finer texture, heavier crust, browner color, and eggier flavor. Additional whites make the texture of a souffle airier; it has greater volume before baking, but not so much when cooked, and delicate flavors seem to come through more readily.

Folding whites with sauce should be done in two steps. Fold in the first addition of whites thoroughly; this lightens the sauce so the remaining whites can be folded in with minimum loss of air. If sauce isn't well blended with the first addition of whites, you may find dense, solid streaks in the baked souffle. If you like, you can create a marbled effect by not completely blending in the second addition of whites.

A souffle dish helps the mixture attain the classic stand-above-the-dish look, but you can use any buttered container of the proper capacity (in rounded containers, the souffle spreads out rather than upward). Fill the dish ¾ full for best appearance. If mixture fills the container completely, fold in place a light foil collar to support the souffle and prevent its overflowing as it bakes. After souffle is partially set, gently slip off the collar so the sides will brown.

Oven times and temperatures can vary according to taste. The ideal temperatures appear to be from 350° to 375°; at very high temperatures a souffle bakes so fast it almost looks stretched where the surface breaks; in addition, the color is deep brown and the interior is much moister than the sides. At low temperatures the souffle sets very evenly throughout and is a light brown.

Appearance and touch are good guides to whether or not a souffle is done—the cracks should look fairly dry and the top should feel firm when lightly tapped. You can test by carefully inserting a long wooden skewer through a surface crack (*don't puncture top; it might fall*); when it comes out clean the souffle is set. There is a school of thought, though, that advocates baking the souffle only until the outer edges are firm and the center is still soft, creating a self-sauce for the souffle. The center will quake slightly at this point, usually in ⅔ to ¾ of the time suggested for a firm souffle.

To start a souffle ahead of time, prepare the sauce, separate the eggs, and butter the dish. To complete preparation, heat the oven, reheat the sauce, add yolks, and proceed as recipe directs. You can leave a baked souffle in the oven as long as 5 minutes without disaster.

Onion Souffle

Slowly cooked onions provide much of the moisture as well as the flavor of the souffle; a sprinkling of nuts makes a crunchy topping.

        3 large onions
        3 tablespoons butter or margarine
        2 tablespoons all-purpose flour
    ½ teaspoon salt
    ⅛ teaspoon pepper
    ½ cup milk
        6 eggs, separated
        2 tablespoons chopped nuts such as
                almonds, walnuts, or pecans

Finely chop onions. Melt butter in a frying pan over medium heat; add onions, cover, and cook until onions are limp and most of the liquid has evaporated (about 20 minutes). Add flour, salt, and pepper, and stir until well blended. Remove from heat and gradually stir in milk. Return to heat and cook, stirring, until thick. (This much can be done ahead; cover and refrigerate; then reheat, stirring.)

Remove hot onion sauce from heat and stir in egg yolks. Beat egg whites until they hold short, distinct, moist-looking peaks. Fold half the beaten whites into onion mixture and then fold in remaining whites as thoroughly as you like.

Pour into a buttered 1½ to 2-quart souffle dish or casserole, or 6 small (1-cup size) dishes. Sprinkle with nuts. Bake large souffle in a 375° oven for 25 to 30 minutes or until center is firm when tapped. Bake small souffles in a 350° oven for 20 to 25 minutes. Makes 4 servings.

Sour Cream Pimento Souffle

Sour cream adds a smooth tanginess to this pimento-streaked souffle.

        4 tablespoons butter or margarine
        4 tablespoons all-purpose flour
    ½ teaspoon salt
    ⅛ teaspoon *each* paprika and dry mustard
    ¾ cup milk
    ¾ cup sour cream
        2 cans (4 oz. *each*) sliced pimentos, drained
        8 egg yolks
        6 egg whites

Melt butter in frying pan and stir in flour, salt, paprika, and mustard. Gradually and smoothly stir in milk, then sour cream; cook, stirring, until thickened. Blend in pimentos. Stir in egg yolks and remove from heat.

Beat egg whites until they hold short, distinct, moist-looking peaks. Fold half the whites smoothly into souffle. Pour mixture into a buttered 2-quart casserole (may be wide and shallow, or deep with fairly straight sides). At this point you can chill souffle for as long as 2 hours (extra yolks give added stability). With tip of knife or spoon, lightly etch a circle on surface of souffle, an inch or so in from the rim if you want souffle to form the classic topknot.

Bake in a 375° oven for 25 to 30 minutes or until the souffle is nicely browned and feels firm when lightly tapped in center (interior should be moist). Makes 6 servings.

Cut Back on Quantities

The American cook's habit (shared by many restaurants) is undue generosity. If the ½-pound meat serving is your standard, consider reducing it. Most diet advisers say this is really a bit too much; 4 or 5-ounce servings are sensible and thrifty.

Lentil Soup with Lemon

From Lebanon comes this chard-filled, lemony legume soup. Enjoy it as an entree accompanied by cucumbers with yogurt or sour cream.

        1 package (12 oz. or 1¾ cups) lentils
            Water
        4 beef bouillon cubes
        1 medium-size baking potato
            About 1½ pounds (or 2 bunches) Swiss
                chard
        1 medium-size onion, finely chopped
        6 tablespoons olive oil or salad oil
        1 cup chopped coriander or 1 cup chopped
                parsley (or 4 tablespoons dried cori-
                ander leaves)
        3 cloves garlic, minced or pressed
            Salt
    ¼ teaspoon pepper
    ½ teaspoon ground cumin seed
        3 tablespoons lemon juice
            Fresh lemon slices

Sort through lentils and discard any extraneous material. Rinse and drain lentils and place them in a 5-quart kettle with 7 cups water and the bouillon cubes; cover and bring to a simmer.

Peel potato and cut into about ½-inch pieces, add to simmering mixture. Wash and drain chard; slice in ½-inch-wide strips and add to soup. Simmer, covered, until lentils are tender (about 45 minutes).

In a frying pan, cook onion over medium heat in oil, stirring often, until onion is soft and golden (15 to 20 minutes). Add about ¾ cup coriander and the garlic to onions to cook for 1 or 2 minutes.

Add onion mixture to soup during last 5 minutes of cooking. Stir in salt to taste, pepper, cumin, lemon juice, and water if needed to thin soup to desired consistency. Serve with reserved coriander and the lemon slices. Makes about 10 cups or 5 or 6 servings.

Do Some Experimenting

When you try alternatives, keep in mind their relative protein values compared to meat. A ¼-pound serving of most meat, fish, or poultry has 20 to 30 grams of protein. Other good protein sources: ½ cup cottage cheese, 15 grams; two eggs, 14; two glasses milk, 17; two chunks (1-inch cubes) Cheddar cheese, 14.

Other foods have much less protein: a slice of bread has 1 or 2 grams; so has a serving of vegetables and most cereals. The Food and Drug Administration has revised its recommended daily allowance for protein downward in recent years; its tables now suggest 56 grams per day for a man, 46 for a woman.

Baked Lentils and Cheese

Lentils, like beans and other legumes, are rich in protein, but lentils cook more quickly. Here, baked into a casserole, they blend deliciously with vegetables and herbs. Lots of Cheddar cheese is melted over them at the last minute.

1 package (12 oz. or 1¾ cups) lentils
  Water
1 bay leaf
1 teaspoon salt
¼ teaspoon pepper
⅛ teaspoon *each* marjoram leaves, rubbed sage, and thyme leaves
2 large onions, chopped
2 cloves garlic, minced or pressed
1 can (1 lb.) tomatoes
2 large carrots, thinly sliced
½ cup thinly sliced celery
1 medium-size green pepper, seeded and chopped
2 tablespoons finely chopped parsley
3 cups (about ¾ lb.) shredded sharp Cheddar cheese

Sort through lentils, discarding any extraneous material. Rinse and drain lentils and place them in a shallow baking dish (about 9 by 13 inches). Mix in 2 cups water, bay, salt, pepper, marjoram, sage, thyme, onions, garlic, and tomatoes with their liquid. Cover and bake in a 375° oven for 30 minutes.

Uncover; stir in carrots and celery. Bake, covered, for 40 minutes more or until vegetables and lentils are tender. Stir in green pepper and parsley. Sprinkle cheese on top; bake, uncovered, for 5 minutes or until cheese melts. Makes 6 servings.

Comparing Protein in Beans and Beef

A pound of dried beans cooked makes about 5 cups—6 or more main-dish servings, depending upon how they are prepared; the addition of meat, cheese, and other protein foods extends the number of portions. White beans and red (or the brown ones) both contain about 100 grams protein per pound; soybeans contain about 150 grams protein per pound. A pound of lean ground beef contains about 90 grams protein and makes 3 or 4 servings.

Refried Beans with Cheese

Refried beans are usually relegated to a side-dish role, but when well fortified with cheese, they are not only very good tasting but hearty enough to make a meal. Serve the beans in warm flour tortillas, and turn tortillas into tacos by adding chile sauce or taco sauce, chopped tomatoes, and shredded lettuce.

1 pound dried pinto beans
  Water
1 pound jack cheese, shredded
  Crushed hot red peppers
  Salt
½ to 1 cup (¼ to ½ lb.) butter, margarine,
  or lard

Sort through beans and discard any extraneous material; rinse beans and drain. Combine beans and 8 cups water in a kettle. Cover and simmer until beans are tender; start checking after 1 hour (it may take up to an hour more). Drain beans, add cheese, and mash thoroughly together. Add hot red peppers and salt to taste. Heat ½ cup butter in a large frying pan, add bean mixture, and cook over medium heat, stirring and scraping frequently, for about 30 minutes to develop refried flavor; add up to ½ cup more butter as needed to prevent sticking. Makes 6 to 8 servings.

Soybean Soup, Bistro-style

Soybeans pureed with leeks and other flavorful vegetables make a soup that has the character of soups served in Parisian sidewalk cafes.

1 cup dried soybeans
6 medium-size leeks (or 2 medium-size
  onions, chopped)
3 tablespoons butter or margarine
1 small onion, chopped
1 cup sliced celery
½ cup chopped carrot
1 medium-size turnip, peeled and diced
1 can (14 oz.) or 2 cups regular-strength
  beef broth
⅛ teaspoon thyme leaves
  Salt and pepper
  About 1 cup milk or half-and-half (light
  cream)
¼ cup finely chopped watercress or parsley
  Lemon wedges

Soak and cook soybeans (as directed in Two Ways to Cook Soybeans, at right); reserve 2 cups of the cooking liquid. Trim root ends and tough outer leaves from leeks; slit each lengthwise and rinse well between layers; then thinly slice. In a 5-quart kettle, melt butter over medium heat; add leeks and onion (or use all onion),

celery and carrot. Cook, stirring, until onion is soft. Add turnip, soybeans, reserved cooking liquid, beef broth, and thyme. Cover and simmer for about 45 minutes or until flavors are well blended.

Pour about ⅓ of the mixture at a time into a blender and whirl until smooth; repeat until all the mixture is pureed. Return soup to kettle. Season to taste with salt and pepper, stir in milk (to achieve desired consistency), and reheat (do not boil). Garnish with watercress and lemon wedges. Makes about 2 quarts or 4 to 6 servings.

Two Ways to Cook Soybeans

You can cook soybeans either conventionally or under pressure. Sort through dried soybeans and discard any extraneous material. Wash and drain beans. To cook beans you need 5 cups water for each 1 cup beans.

To cook over direct heat, place washed beans and water in a kettle and bring to a boil; simmer 5 minutes. Remove beans from heat, cover, and let soak 2 hours. (Or you can simply soak beans at least 6 hours or overnight.)

Drain soaked beans, reserving water. Discard loose, fibrous bean skins. Return water to beans, bring to a boil, cover, and simmer for about 3 hours or until beans are tender. (Length of cooking time can vary a great deal, so start testing for tenderness after 2 hours of cooking.) Add water if needed to keep beans from sticking; stir occasionally.

To cook in a pressure cooker, place washed beans and water in the pan. Cover pan and, following manufacturer's directions, cook at 15 pounds pressure for 40 minutes. Cool pan quickly under cold running water; remove lid (if beans are not as tender as you like, cook additionally at simmer as long as needed). When cool, drain beans, reserving liquid. Discard loose, fibrous bean skins.

Use beans and liquid as directed in the recipes on pages 77 and 78. Any extra bean liquid can go into soups, broths, or sauces.

Marinated Soybean Salad

Indigenous to China and Japan, soybeans have such an intriguing nutlike flavor and such a wealth of nutrition that they are assuming an important place in western cuisine. A cheese and egg garnish supplements the nutrition of this tart and tasty bean salad.

(Recipe continued on next page)

1 cup dried soybeans
¼ cup finely chopped parsley
1 small green pepper, seeded and finely chopped
2 green onions, thinly sliced
⅓ cup olive oil or salad oil
3 tablespoons wine vinegar
½ teaspoon salt
¼ teaspoon Dijon mustard
⅛ teaspoon *each* pepper and basil leaves
Butter lettuce leaves
2 hard-cooked eggs, quartered
1 medium-size tomato, cut in wedges
About 4 ounces sharp Cheddar cheese, cut in thin strips

Soak and cook soybeans (as directed in Two Ways to Cook Soybeans, page 77). Drain soybeans, reserving liquid for other uses, such as soup. Combine soybeans, parsley, green pepper, and green onions. Blend together oil, vinegar, salt, mustard, pepper, and basil; pour over bean mixture and mix well. Cover and refrigerate for 4 hours or overnight; stir several times. Heap beans in lettuce-lined bowl; garnish with eggs, tomato, cheese. Makes 6 servings.

Tofu and Chicken Stir-fry

A very little chicken goes a long way when teamed up with tofu. Before you start to cook, have all the ingredients assembled and cut as directed.

1 tablespoon sesame seed
¼ cup salad oil
About ¾ pound boneless, skinned chicken (light or dark meat), cut in ¼-inch-thick slices
2 cloves garlic, minced or pressed
1 tablespoon grated fresh ginger root
1 large onion, cut in half crosswise, quartered lengthwise, layers separated
½ pound small mushrooms, quartered
1 cup thinly sliced carrots
½ cup chopped green onion
½ cup chopped coriander (or 2 tablespoons dried coriander leaves)
½ pound edible pea pods (ends and strings removed) or 1 package (about 7 oz.) thawed frozen edible pea pods
About 1 pound medium-firm or hard tofu, well drained and cut in ½-inch cubes
Cooking sauce (directions follow)

Place wok or wide frying pan over high heat. Add sesame seeds and stir until golden. Pour out of pan and set aside.

Heat oil in pan, add chicken, and cook, stirring, until chicken starts to turn opaque (about 1 minute). Add garlic, ginger, and onion and cook, stirring, 1 more minute. Then add mushrooms and carrots and cook, stirring, another minute (vegetables will be only slightly cooked). Add green onion, coriander, peas, tofu, and cooking sauce. Cook, stirring gently, until sauce boils and thickens. Pour into a serving dish and sprinkle with sesame seed. Makes 4 or 5 servings.

Cooking sauce. Blend 1 tablespoon cornstarch, ¼ teaspoon pepper, ¼ cup dry Sherry, 2 tablespoons vinegar, and 3 tablespoons soy sauce.

Fried Tofu Salad with Peanuts

An intriguing salad combines deep-fried tofu puffs with fresh vegetables and peanuts, served in a sweet-hot peanut butter dressing. Round out the meal with omelets (page 71), if you like.

½ pound bean sprouts
1 large cucumber, peeled and thinly sliced
3 green onions, thinly sliced (include some tops)
½ cup minced carrot
½ cup finely chopped salted peanuts
3 Japanese-style deep-fried tofu puffs (about 2 oz.) cut in 1-inch cubes; or 15 Chinese-style deep-fried tofu puffs (about 5 oz.)
Peanut dressing (recipe follows)

In salad bowl combine bean sprouts, cucumber, onions, carrot, salted peanuts, tofu. Pour in dressing and mix. Makes 4 to 6 servings.

Peanut dressing. Whirl smooth in a blender ½ small onion, 2 cloves garlic, 2 tablespoons brown sugar, ¼ teaspoon crushed hot red pepper, 3 tablespoons *each* soy sauce and lemon juice, and 2 tablespoons peanut butter.

Tofu Watercress Soup

Raw or leftover cooked meat can be used in this soup; slices are so thin that even uncooked meat will be done in moments.

- 2 cans (about 14 oz. *each*) or 3½ to 4 cups regular-strength chicken or beef broth
- ¼ teaspoon ground ginger
  About 1 tablespoon soy sauce
- 1 clove garlic, minced or pressed
- 1 cup chopped watercress
- 1 cup thinly sliced cooked chicken, turkey, beef, or other meat; or ½ pound uncooked lean boneless beef, sliced in thin strips
- ½ pound soft or medium-firm tofu, well drained and cut in ½-inch cubes

Bring to a boil the broth with ginger, 1 tablespoon soy, and garlic. Add watercress, meat, and tofu; simmer about 3 minutes to heat ingredients thoroughly. Add soy to taste. Makes 4 servings.

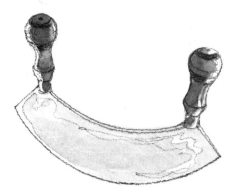

Tofu—Alternative from the Orient

The search for inexpensive alternatives to meat is leading cooks to an oriental protein food known as soybean curd or, by the more common Japanese name, tofu.

Tofu may initially seem strange in appearance and custardlike texture, but it's quick and convenient to prepare, and because of its mild, almost neutral, taste, it readily assumes the flavors of the ingredients with which it is cooked. The remarkable versatility of tofu makes it useful in a wide variety of dishes, from appetizers and soups to main dishes and desserts.

Tofu is made with ground soybeans and water, cooked until a milky liquid is extracted. The liquid is drained off and a coagulant is added to set the liquid, making the basic curd.

Fresh tofu appears in several different forms, mainly distinguished by their degrees of firmness. Extremely soft tofu is known as *fresh soybean pudding.* The curd in its next basic form is simply called *soft tofu.* The most widely available form of tofu is *medium-firm,* made by draining excess liquid from the curd and compressing it. *Hard tofu* is drained and compressed even more.

All four of these tofu types are interchangeable as far as flavor goes; the only distinction is texture. Soft tofu is preferred for soups; hard tofu is best for stir-fry dishes, as it holds its shape.

Tofu is also sold in two partially cooked styles. Fried soybean curd is highly compressed tofu fried in hot oil until it reaches the proper doneness—just until the exterior browns, for *raw-fried tofu,* or until puffy and hollow, for *deep-fried tofu puffs.*

Tofu's nutritional value. The more concentrated the form of tofu, the higher the protein content. No tofu product contains as much protein by weight as meat, fish, or poultry, but tofu can still contribute substantial amounts of high-quality protein, especially when used with meats in main dishes or added to soup or salads.

A quarter-pound of medium-firm tofu (the only tofu product we know of that has been chemically analyzed) supplies about as much protein as an extra-large egg—about 8 grams. Its calcium about equals that of milk, and tofu is low in fat. In comparison with other protein sources, it is low in cost.

Always drain water-packed styles of tofu before using. Gently turn tofu into a colander to drain for about 20 minutes. Save the container; it is ideal for storing leftover curd. To store leftover tofu, add enough fresh water to cover curd in tub, cover tightly and refrigerate; do not freeze. Fresh tofu or raw-fried tofu will keep up to 10 days; it will smell sour if it has deteriorated. Deep-fried tofu puffs can be frozen and kept up to a month if they're well wrapped; when refrigerated, this style will keep for about 2 weeks.

Medium-firm tofu is found with increasing frequency in supermarkets, but you'll probably have to shop in oriental food markets for the other kinds of tofu.

Vegetables That Add a Special Touch

Simply cooked vegetables—ranging from artichokes and asparagus to yams and zucchini—bring so much color and freshness to a meal that the inclination is to accept these assets and go no further. That inclination needs to be nudged.

In this chapter we take a purposeful look at the more complex potential of vegetables: ways to develop their flavors individually—by slow-cooking cabbage or onions, or crisp-frying onions; or ways to use the flavors of vegetables together—in French ratatouille, or Dutch hutspot. The savory, nourishing quality of vegetables is also fortified by eggs, cheese, or meat broth in some tasty ways—topping for broccoli, the custard in which thinly sliced potatoes bake, or an elegant spinach pie.

You'll also find dishes using the grains—wheat, rice, and polenta (the coarsely ground cornmeal), as well as tender egg dumplings to serve as you would one of the starchy dishes.

In fact, consider some of these dishes as entrees, if you find them sufficiently satisfying.

Bonuses are directions for growing—right in the kitchen—coriander, an herb frequently called for in this book, and all kinds of useful sprouts.

Toasted Cabbage

Plain and simple, this old Hungarian way of frying cabbage slowly and gently transforms the humble vegetable into a subtly flavored complement for various pork dishes, chicken, even scrambled eggs. It's almost more a relish than a vegetable.

    1   very large (about 3 lb.) green cabbage
    1   tablespoon salt
    ½   cup (¼ lb.) butter or margarine
    3   tablespoons sugar
    ¼   teaspoon freshly ground black pepper

Remove core and finely chop cabbage. Mix cabbage with salt and let stand at room temperature for at least 30 minutes. Place cabbage in a colander and rinse briefly under cold running water; then squeeze out liquid.

Melt butter in a wide frying pan and add cabbage. Cook, uncovered, over medium-low heat for about 30 minutes, stirring frequently. When cabbage becomes limp and turns a brighter color, add sugar and pepper. Continue cooking until cabbage takes on an amber color and a few particles begin to brown lightly and look crisp; frequently stir gently.

If made ahead, cover and chill; reheat in a frying pan over moderate heat. Makes about 3½ cups or 6 to 8 servings.

Growing Coriander

Coriander is a distinctly flavored herb used frequently in this book; it is also known as "Chinese parsley" and "cilantro." In some parts of the country, coriander is available in supermarkets and in oriental and Mexican food stores. But it may be necessary to grow your own and this is *easy* to do—using coriander seed from the spice shelf of the grocery store. Or you can buy the seeds in nurseries, or order from seed catalogs. Spring and early fall (for mild climates) are good sowing times for outdoor plants; window gardens can be started any time for a continuing year-round supply.

Plant in full sun, or part shade in hot places. Prepare the ground as you would for any flower or vegetable. In containers, use a lightweight planting mix.

Sow seeds ¼ to ½ inch deep in rows 6 inches apart; you can poke holes for seeds with a pencil or small stick. Space as close as an inch apart, but when seedlings are 2 inches tall, thin them to stand about 4 inches apart; use the thinnings in the kitchen. Water the soil lightly right after planting and keep it damp until seeds sprout— usually inside of 2 weeks. Seedlings soon send down deep tap roots, making transplanting difficult.

Coriander has no special water requirements and usually needs no fertilizer unless you grow more than one crop in the same bed or container.

There are two ways to keep coriander coming continuously. One way is to sow a new batch of seeds about every 2 weeks. In 6 or 8 weeks, when plants reach 4 to 6 inches tall, pull them out— leaves, stems, roots, and all. This method works best in areas where heat speeds up coriander's season.

The other way: Cut off young tender leaves and stems a few at a time—as you would pick chives or parsley. This encourages more tender new growth, thwarts seed-setting, and prolongs the plant's season. Start cutting when the plant is 4 to 6 inches tall; don't let it get much bigger or you won't be able to stop it from seeding. Cut only the tip leaves and side stems. Cutting too far back or removing the inner stems may kill the plant. If plant grows tough or blooms, pull out and replace.

Danish Crisp Onions

The Danes use their special version of fried onions with a free hand to dress servings of simply cooked meats, fish, vegetables, or sandwiches. You can make your own chewy-crisp, naturally sweet onion shreds and store them in refrigerator or freezer, ready to use.

    4   large (about 1½ lb.) white-fleshed onions
    ½   cup all-purpose flour, unsifted
        Salad oil

Peel onions and slice thinly. Separate slices into rings and place in a large bag with flour. Shake to coat rings evenly with flour.

In a deep 3-quart pan, on high heat, bring 1½ inches salad oil to 300°. Add about ⅓ of the floured onions to the oil; cook about 10 minutes or until onions are golden brown. The temperature of the oil will come back up to 275° as the onions start to brown; regulate heat to maintain this temperature. Stir onions frequently. With a slotted spoon, lift browned onions from oil and drain on absorbent material; lift out particles that brown faster than others to prevent them from scorching.

Cook remaining onions in the hot oil, following this same procedure. Serve onions warm or cold. When completely cooled, package airtight for later use. Store in the refrigerator up to 3 days or freeze up to 1 month.

Serve right from the refrigerator or freezer. Or to reheat, spread in a single layer in a shallow pan and place in a 350° oven for 2 or 3 minutes. Makes about 8 cups or ½ pound; allow about ¼ cup for a serving.

Polenta

In northern Italy, a staple dish is polenta (poh-*len*-tah), made of coarsely ground cornmeal. Similar to cornmeal mush, but with more texture and a special nutlike flavor, it takes the place of rice or potatoes. Serve it plain or pan fried.

  3 cups water
  2 chicken bouillon cubes or ½ teaspoon salt
     (or omit water and bouillon and use 3 cups
     regular-strength chicken broth)
  1 cup polenta
    About 3 tablespoons butter or margarine
 ½ cup shredded jack, mozzarella, or
    Cheddar cheese (optional)

In a deep, heavy, 3-quart pan, bring to a boil water and bouillon. Slowly stir in the polenta. Reduce heat and cook, stirring, until very thick (about 7 minutes). Remove from heat and stir in 2 tablespoons butter or margarine until melted. Spoon onto plates and top servings with 1 more tablespoon butter and the shredded cheese. Makes 4 servings.

Pan-fried polenta. Cook polenta according to preceding directions; stir in butter. Spread in a well-buttered 8-inch square pan. Cool in pan 30 minutes and then invert onto a flat surface. Use polenta warm or wrap and refrigerate up to 4 days. To serve, cut polenta into 4 squares. Melt 3 tablespoons butter or margarine in a frying pan over medium heat. Add polenta and cook until crusty on both sides. Top each portion with about 1 tablespoon grated Parmesan cheese or shredded jack or mozzarella cheese.

Eat with the Season

Choose foods priced to reflect a current plentifulness, and, generally, best quality. This applies not only to meat, poultry, and fish, but to fruits and vegetables as well.

Ratatouille

This French vegetable classic is an easy-to-make stew of eggplant, squash, bell peppers, tomatoes, onions, and garlic simmered in their own juices. You can cook ratatouille (rah-tah-*too*-ee) quickly over direct heat or bake it slowly to preserve the shape and texture of the vegetable pieces. Either way, it's best when made ahead so the flavors can mellow and mingle. Serve it hot, at room temperature, or cold—either with a meat dish or as a refreshing vegetable entree.

    About ½ cup olive oil or salad oil
  2 large onions, sliced
  2 large cloves garlic, minced or pressed
  1 medium-size (1¼ to 1½ lb.) eggplant, cut
     in ½-inch cubes
  6 medium-size zucchini, thickly sliced
  2 medium-size green or red bell peppers,
     seeded and cut in chunks
    About 1½ teaspoons salt
  1 teaspoon basil leaves
 ½ cup minced parsley
  4 large tomatoes, cut in chunks
    Parsley
    Sliced tomato (optional)

Heat ¼ cup oil in a large frying pan over high heat. Add onions and garlic and cook, stirring, until onions are soft but not browned. Stir in eggplant, zucchini, peppers, 1½ teaspoons salt, basil, and minced parsley; add a little of the oil as needed to keep the vegetables from sticking. Cover and cook over moderate heat for about 30 minutes; stir occasionally, using a large spatula and turning vegetables to help preserve their shape. If mixture becomes quite soupy during this time, remove cover to allow some of the moisture to escape.

Add tomato chunks to vegetables in pan and stir to blend. Also add more oil if vegetables are sticking. Cover and cook over moderate heat for 15 minutes; stir occasionally. Again, if mixture becomes soupy, remove cover. Ratatouille should have a little free liquid but still be of a good spoon-and-serve consistency. Add more salt if required. Serve ratatouille hot; or cover, chill, and serve cold; or reheat to serve. Garnish with parsley and sliced tomato if desired. Makes 8 to 10 servings.

Ratatouille in the oven. Using the vegetables and seasonings in the preceding recipe, layer all ingredients into a 6-quart casserole, pressing down to make fit if necessary. Drizzle only 4 tablespoons oil over top layer. Cover casserole and bake in a 350° oven for 3 hours. Baste top occasionally with some of the liquid. Uncover during last hour if quite soupy; this method of cooking makes a more moist ratatouille. Mix gently and salt to taste. Serve hot, cool, or reheated. Garnish with parsley and tomato if desired. Makes 8 to 10 servings.

Shredded Zucchini Pancakes

Green flecks of shredded zucchini are laced liberally through these creamy mashed-potato pancakes. Wholesome wheat germ adds a nutty flavor. Serve the thick, golden brown cakes Russian-style —with sour cream and jam—for a meal. Accompany with crisp bacon and a salad of sliced cucumbers and tomatoes.

  2 medium-large baking potatoes (about 1 lb. total)
    About 1 cup water
    About ¾ teaspoon salt
  2 tablespoons butter or margarine
  1 medium-size onion, finely chopped
  4 medium-size (about 1 lb.) zucchini
  3 eggs, beaten slightly
  ½ cup wheat germ, plain or toasted
  ½ cup matzo meal or saltine cracker crumbs
  ¼ teaspoon pepper
    Salad oil and butter or margarine
    Sour cream (optional)
    Fruit or berry jam (optional)

Peel potatoes and cut into ½-inch cubes. Combine in a small pan with ¾ cup water and ¾ teaspoon salt. Cover, bring to a boil, and simmer until potatoes mash easily (15 to 20 minutes). Drain and measure liquid. (You need 2 tablespoons; boil down to this amount or add water, if needed, to make this amount). Add liquid to potatoes and mash smoothly while mixture is still hot, or when cooled.

Meanwhile, melt 2 tablespoons butter, add onion, and cook, stirring occasionally, until onion is soft.

Cut off stem ends and coarsely shred zucchini. Combine with potatoes, onions and butter, eggs,

wheat germ, matzo meal, and pepper. Mix well. Taste; add more salt if needed.

Add 3 or 4 tablespoons *each* salad oil and butter or margarine to a 10 to 12-inch frying pan. Place over medium heat and, when butter is melted, add the potato-zucchini mixture in generous ¼-cup portions; flatten surface to make ¾-inch-thick cakes. Cook until cakes are browned on one side; then turn with a wide spatula and brown on the other side; allow 3 to 5 minutes for each side.

Keep pancakes hot until all are cooked; add more oil and butter or margarine to frying pan as needed. Accompany pancakes with sour cream and jam to spoon onto each portion. Makes about 15 pancakes; allow about 3 for a serving.

Broccoli with Broiled Topping

The same puffy, cheese-flavored sauce that tops broccoli will also dress up cooked cauliflower or green beans.

  1½ to 2 pounds broccoli
    Boiling, salted water
  ½ cup mayonnaise
  ¼ cup freshly grated Parmesan cheese
  2 tablespoons finely chopped parsley
  2 teaspoons lemon juice
  2 egg whites

Trim off tough ends from broccoli and separate into thin spears; rinse well. Drop the broccoli spears into water and cook, uncovered, until just tender when pierced, about 7 minutes. Drain well and arrange in a shallow 1½-quart casserole.

Meanwhile, in a small bowl combine the mayonnaise, Parmesan cheese, parsley, and lemon juice. Beat the egg whites until soft, moist peaks form; fold into the mayonnaise mixture. Spread the topping evenly over the cooked broccoli. Broil 8 to 10 inches below heat until topping is richly browned (about 5 minutes). Serve immediately. Makes 4 to 6 servings.

Two Jobs at Once

Whenever possible, use your oven to cook more than one dish at a time. Bake a vegetable casserole when roasting a piece of meat; or bake a dessert along with a vegetable dish. You save not only effort, but energy—the kind you buy.

Buying Mushrooms in Bulk

Mushrooms are among the more expensive vegetables. But because they contribute a great deal to many dishes, it's worth investigating more practical ways to make use of them.

For example, when mushrooms are at a special price, you might buy them in multiple pound lots, then saute them and freeze in portions you can expect to use in recipes that call for sauteed mushrooms. If a recipe calls for 1 pound of mushrooms, you would use about 1⅔ cups sliced sauteed mushrooms, thawed, adding mushrooms to the dish as directed and omitting the sauteing step. A slightly generous ¾ cup sliced sauteed mushrooms is equal to ½ pound raw mushrooms; a scant ½ cup sliced sauteed mushrooms is equal to ¼ pound raw mushrooms.

To saute mushrooms, wash well (try adding water to mushrooms in plastic bag and gently squeezing from the outside), drain, trim discolored end off stem, then slice mushrooms. Allow 2 tablespoons butter or margarine for each pound of mushrooms; cook, stirring, until liquid is evaporated and mushrooms are limp.

Spinach Pie

Attractive and well seasoned, this vegetable pie goes deliciously with simply prepared meats, especially chicken or turkey. However, the pie is so well supplemented by eggs and cheese that it can qualify as a light main dish as well.

  1 small package (3 oz.) cream cheese, at
     room temperature
  1 cup light cream (half-and-half)
  ½ cup soft bread cubes, lightly packed
  ¼ cup shredded Parmesan cheese
  2 eggs, slightly beaten
  1¼ pounds fresh spinach, cooked (or use 1 cup
     thawed frozen spinach), very well
     drained, and finely chopped
  4 tablespoons butter or margarine
  1 large onion, finely chopped
  ½ pound mushrooms, finely chopped
  1 teaspoon tarragon leaves
     About ¾ teaspoon salt
     Unbaked 9 or 10-inch pastry shell
     (page 92)

Mash cream cheese with a fork and gradually blend in light cream. Add bread cubes, Parmesan cheese, and eggs to cream cheese mixture and beat with a rotary mixer or wire whip to break up bread pieces. Stir in spinach.

Melt butter in a wide frying pan and cook onion and mushrooms until lightly browned and liquid has evaporated, stirring frequently; add tarragon when vegetables are soft. Blend hot vegetables with spinach mixture. Salt to taste. Pour vegetable filling into pastry shell. Bake on lowest rack in a 400° oven for 25 minutes or until crust is well browned. Let stand 10 minutes and cut to serve hot, or let cool and cut to serve. Makes about 6 to 8 servings.

Spinach pie with lattice crust. Make pie as directed above, but make enough pastry for a two-crust 9 or 10-inch pie.

Roll out a little more than half the pastry on a floured board and fit into pan. Pour vegetable mixture into pastry shell.

Roll out remaining pastry on a floured board until about ⅛ inch thick. Cut pastry in strips about ½ inch wide and interlace evenly in a latticework over the filling. Crimp edges of pastry decoratively and bake as directed.

Brown Rice and Sprout Pilaf

At the last moment of cooking, mix fresh sprouts (purchased or grown according to directions on the next page) into this hot pilaf to add a tender crunch and sweetness.

  1 large onion, finely chopped
  1 cup coarsely shredded carrots
  4 tablespoons butter or margarine
  1 cup regular brown rice
  2½ cups regular-strength chicken broth
  2 cups lentil, rye, wheat, or immature mung
     bean sprouts (or 4 cups commercial-size
     bean sprouts)
  ½ cup minced parsley

In a pan, saute onion and carrot in butter until soft. Stir in rice; continue to cook, stirring over medium-high heat, until rice begins to slightly brown. Add chicken broth, cover, and simmer 45 minutes or until rice is tender and liquid is absorbed. Stir in sprouts and parsley and remove from heat. Makes 4 to 6 servings.

Growing Your Own Sprouts

You can have a vegetable garden right in the kitchen when you grow your own edible sprouts from seed. Whether it rains or shines, you can easily, neatly, and quickly get a crop within 2 to 7 days. Use the leafy sprouts as garnish when a bit of attractive greenery will add to the appeal of a dish. Or use the sprouted seeds in salads or with vegetables.

How to grow sprouts

Sprouts come in two basic types. There are tiny ones that you eat when they form green leaves: alfalfa and mustard. And there are larger ones that you eat before the leaves open or turn green: mung bean, wheat, and lentil.

You sprout both kinds in almost the same way. Discard broken or unhealthy-looking seeds. Soak whole seeds in about three times their volume of water until they are saturated—tiny seeds become saturated in a few hours; large ones take overnight. Drain off water that hasn't been absorbed and keep seeds in a warm place (68° or slightly warmer).

Arrange for growth in containers according to suggestions that follow.

Keep the seeds moist by rinsing or spraying with lukewarm water two to four times a day. When seeds pop, give leafy green sprouts plenty of light. Lentil and wheat can grow in light or dark. Keep mung beans in the dark and water often; otherwise they develop an unpleasant "green" flavor. (Mung sprouts also require constant warmth to look and taste like commercial ones. Many people eliminate difficulties with mung sprouts by using them when ¼ to 1 inch long instead of waiting until they reach the commercial size of 2 to 3 inches.

These immature mung sprouts have a mild legume flavor that brief cooking brings out nicely.)

Sprouts taste best and have most nutrients if you use them soon after they reach mature size. If the leafy sprouts grow in trays, cut the sprouts off close to the base to use. Rinse off loose seed hulls, or use hulls and all.

If it's necessary to store sprouts, drain on absorbent material; then place in an airtight container and refrigerate. Wilt or decay indicates the passing of the sprouts' prime.

You can buy these seeds in quantity at most health food stores; lentils and mustard seed are also commonly sold in grocery stores. If you can't find a particular type of seed in your local store, try a nursery or seed company.

What to sprout seeds in

Shallow dishes with cheesecloth can be used to grow the two green sprouts. Do not use metal containers. Spread one layer of seeds over several thicknesses of cheesecloth or paper towel.

A colander is good for growing any of the larger sprouts. Soak the seeds overnight in another container first; then put them in the colander (not a metal one) and rinse two to four times a day until ready to use. Cover with a towel to reduce evaporation and hold warmth. Rest colander on a plate to catch drain water.

Cleaning sprouters. Regular washing between uses is usually sufficient to clean sprouters, but if mold problems should develop, sterilize by rinsing with a dilute solution of chlorine bleach (1 teaspoon to 1 quart of water) and rinse again with water.

	Growing time	Harvest size	Yield (seed)	Yield (sprouts)	Taste
Alfalfa	3 to 5 days	1½ to 2″	1 tablespoon makes 4 cups		crisp, mild, grassy
Mustard	5 to 6 days	1½ to 2″	1 tablespoon makes 2 cups		pleasant bite, similar to mustard greens
Lentil	2 to 4 days	¾ to 1½″	1 cup makes 6 cups		mildly spicy, fresh vegetable flavor and crunch, slightly starchy when raw
Mung bean	1 to 5 days (immature) 5 to 7 days (commercial size)	¼″ and up 2 to 3″	depends on harvest size; 1 cup makes 5 to 12 cups		pleasant legume flavor, crunchy bland, crunchy
Wheat	2 days	¼″	1 cup makes 4 cups		sweet, nutty, chewy

Wheat Berry Pilaf

Wheat berries are the whole wheat kernels with only the chaff removed; when soaked, then boiled, the round grains have a slightly resilient texture and a sweet, nutlike flavor that makes a delicious base for a pilaf. Here you combine the berries with mushrooms and zucchini, season them with basil, and then give them a broiled topping of melted cheese. You can cook the wheat ahead of time and refrigerate for up to a week, or freeze it to have on hand.

  ¼ cup salad oil (may be half butter or margarine)
  1 medium-size onion, chopped
  ½ pound mushrooms, thinly sliced
  2 teaspoons beef stock base (or 2 cubes beef bouillon)
  ½ cup hot water (or liquid drained from wheat, below)
  ½ teaspoon basil leaves
  ¼ teaspoon pepper
  3 cups cooked, drained wheat berries (directions follow)
  2 medium-size zucchini
    Salt
  1 cup shredded Cheddar or jack cheese
    About 2 tablespoons minced parsley

Heat oil in a large frying pan over medium heat. Cook onion and mushrooms until limp and until liquid has evaporated. Add stock base and water to pan with basil, pepper, and wheat berries; stir well. Cover and bring to a simmer. Thinly slice zucchini and stir into wheat. Cover and simmer until wheat is heated through and liquid is absorbed (about 10 minutes).

Season to taste with salt; then transfer mixture to a shallow 2-quart casserole that can go under the broiler. Sprinkle with cheese; broil about 4 inches from heat until cheese is melted (about 2 minutes). Sprinkle with parsley for garnish. Makes about 6 servings.

Cooked wheat berries: In a large pan, combine 1 cup wheat berries and 5 cups water. Cover and let stand at least 8 hours. (Or cover pan, bring to a boil over highest heat, boil 2 minutes, remove from heat, cover, and let stand for 1 hour.)

Without draining the wheat, bring to a boil over high heat. Reduce heat and simmer until tender (about 1½ hours). Drain well (save the liquid if desired); cool. Cover and store in the refrigerator or freeze (thaw before using). Makes about 3 cups.

Swiss Potatoes

Bake a roast or chicken when you cook these potatoes, to make energy-wise use of the oven.

  1 clove garlic, peeled and halved
    About 2½ tablespoons butter or margarine
  3 tablespoons vinegar or lemon juice
    Water
  5 large new potatoes (about 2½ lb. total)
    Salt, pepper, and ground nutmeg
  ¾ cup thinly sliced green onions
  2 cups shredded Swiss cheese
  1½ cups milk or light cream (half-and-half)
  1 egg, slightly beaten

Rub a shallow 2-quart baking dish liberally with garlic; then generously coat with about 2 teaspoons butter.

In a bowl combine vinegar and water. Peel potatoes (or leave skins on) and cut into very thin slices; place in the water until all are sliced (to keep potatoes from darkening).

Drain potatoes well and arrange about ¼ of the slices in an even layer in the prepared dish; sprinkle lightly with salt, pepper, and nutmeg; then top with about ¼ of the onions and ¼ of the cheese. Repeat layers, ending with cheese. Scald milk; pour slowly into egg, beating constantly until blended; then slowly pour over and around potatoes. Dot top with remaining butter. Bake, uncovered, in a 350° oven for about 1½ hours or until potatoes are tender when pierced. Makes 6 to 8 servings.

Hutspot

A creamy swirl of mashed potatoes laced, Dutch-fashion, with golden flecks of carrot and onion makes an impressively tasty dish, despite its humble ingredients. For maximum flavor, boil potatoes in broth instead of water; then serve with gravy or juices of meat.

  4 to 6 tablespoons butter or margarine
  2 large onions, coarsely chopped
  2 pounds (about 4 medium-size) baking potatoes
  1 pound (4 to 6 large) carrots or parsnips
  3 cups water or regular-strength beef or chicken broth
    About ⅓ cup milk or light cream (half-and-half)
    Salt and pepper
    Additional butter, gravy, or meat juice

Melt butter in a wide frying pan over medium-high heat; add onion and cook, stirring occasionally, until limp and golden, about 15 minutes. When cooked, keep warm.

Meanwhile, peel potatoes and carrots and cut in about 1-inch chunks. Place vegetables in a 3 to 4-quart pan and add water or broth. Bring to a boil, cover, and simmer 20 minutes or until pieces pierce easily.

Drain (reserve liquid for soups or other cooking) and mash vegetables smoothly, adding ⅓ cup (or more) milk or cream until of desired creamy consistency. Stir in onion mixture and season with salt and pepper. Serve hot with additional butter, gravy, or meat juices. Makes 6 servings.

Risotto

Risotto is rice cooked in a way that develops a creamy, flowing consistency. Even in its plainest form, seasoned only with a little onion, garlic, and cheese, risotto is a distinctive dish to serve either as a first course or with an entree.

About 3 tablespoons butter or margarine
About 2 tablespoons olive oil or salad oil
1 small or medium-size onion, chopped
1 clove garlic, minced or pressed
1 cup long grain rice or pearl rice
About 3½ cups regular-strength chicken or beef broth, heated to simmering
Salt
½ cup freshly grated or shredded Parmesan, Asiago, or Romano cheese
Additional freshly grated or shredded Parmesan, Asiago, or Romano cheese

Heat 2 tablespoons of the butter and the olive oil together in pan (about 2-qt. size) or 10-inch frying pan with a tight-fitting lid. Add the chopped onion and cook over medium heat until soft and golden, stirring. Add garlic and rice and stir until the rice is milky and opaque in appearance, about 3 minutes.

Next add 1 cup of the broth, reduce heat, cover, and simmer until most of the liquid has been absorbed, about 10 minutes. Add remaining hot broth in 2 or 3 additions, each time stirring lightly with a fork; cook until rice is tender and most of the liquid has been absorbed (about 20 to 25 minutes longer). Exact amount of liquid needed and cooking time vary with rice and cooking pan you use; also, pearl rice cooks a little faster than long grain. Taste; add salt if needed.

Remove from heat and add ¼ cup of the cheese

and remaining 1 tablespoon butter; mix lightly with fork. Pour into a serving dish and top with remaining ¼ cup cheese. Pass additional cheese at the table. Makes 4 to 6 servings.

Spatzle

Spatzle are the tiny egg dumplings served in such mid-European countries as Austria and Hungary. To make them, you rub a soupy batter through a spatzle maker or slotted spoon. This causes the batter to break into little droplets as it falls into boiling water. The water firms them almost at once. Spatzle can be frozen, if you want to make a good supply. Serve these dumplings as you would pasta or rice.

3 eggs
Salt
Water
1¾ cups all-purpose flour, unsifted
2 or 3 tablespoons butter or margarine

Beat together until very well blended the eggs, ½ teaspoon salt, ½ cup water, and flour.

Hold a large slotted spoon (or spatzle maker) several inches above a wide 4 to 5-quart pan containing about 5 inches of rapidly boiling, salted water. Partially fill spoon with the batter and then force batter through the holes with a wooden spoon or rubber spatula, breaking up strands as they fall into the water.

When each addition of the spatzle has returned to the surface (stir if necessary), cook an additional 10 seconds; then skim spatzle from water and drain. Melt 2 tablespoons butter in a pan and mix in spatzle as they are cooked. Repeat procedure until all batter is cooked.

Spatzle may be reheated with the butter (stir over moderate heat) and served at once; or cooled and packed in serving-size packages and refrigerated 3 or 4 days, or frozen for later use. Makes about 3½ cups or 4 to 6 servings.

Brown butter spatzle. Heat 1 to 2 tablespoons butter or margarine in a wide frying pan until it just begins to brown. Stir in one half to a full recipe's worth of cooked spatzle and heat through, browning lightly. Serve plain or garnish with shredded Parmesan cheese, minced parsley, or chopped chives.

A Sweet Finale

Bringing a meal to a sweet, yet economical, conclusion can be done in a number of good-tasting ways. A most deliciously effortless style is simply to offer a basket of fresh fruit to peel, cut, slice, sweeten as needed.

But fruit is a dessert with endless possibilities—some appear in the following pages; many others appear in menu suggestions accompanying other recipes throughout the book.

Sometimes, though, a more elaborate dessert is called for. In this chapter, you'll find the emphasis is on wholesomeness—pies made with fruit or cereals, breads sweetened by fruit and honey, egg creations, rice pudding with a flair, and ice cream that brings down the house.

Gingered Tropical Fruits

Arrange fruits on a tray or on individual plates; pass the sauce to add to taste. Or you can use just sliced oranges or bananas with the sauce; you'll need 6 to 8 of either fruit.

 1 small pineapple (or half a large one)
 2 oranges
 1 papaya
 3 bananas
 1 lemon
   Mint leaves
   Ginger sauce (directions follow)

Peel pineapple, oranges, and papaya with a knife. Slice pineapple and oranges into thin rounds; seed papaya and cut in lengthwise slices. Peel bananas and cut in slanting thick slices; sprinkle with lemon juice to prevent darkening.

Arrange fruit attractively on a platter and garnish with mint leaves. Serve sauce in a small bowl. Invite people to make their own servings. Makes 6 to 8 servings.

Ginger sauce. Blend 1 cup sour cream and 1½ tablespoons *each* honey and chopped candied ginger; chill, covered.

The Classic Dessert Is Fruit

A survey of fresh fruits—both the seasonal ones and those that are on the scene most of the time—indicates the variety of ways you can easily and healthfully end a meal throughout the year.

Almost any time you'll find apples and pears (though the varieties change), oranges, grapefruit, bananas, pineapple, papaya, and kiwi.

But in the summer the choices are dazzling: strawberries, raspberries, blackberries, loganberries, ollalieberries, blueberries, gooseberries, currants, cherries, peaches, nectarines, plums, mangoes, grapes, watermelon, cantaloupe, and Crenshaw, honeydew, and Persian melons.

In the fall, melons and grapes and some stone fruits continue, supplemented by winter pears, winter apples, persimmons, pomegranates (and nuts, if you class them as fruit).

With the coolness of winter come the tangerines, mandarins, oranges, and grapefruit.

Spring starts the cycle again, with strawberries reappearing and apples, pears, and citrus hanging on from harvest time.

Coupling fruits with appropriate cheese is the classic way to give even more dimension to fruit for dessert.

Apple-filled Crepes

If you have crepes on hand in your freezer, this elegant dessert is an exceptionally quick one.

 5 tablespoons butter or margarine
 4 cups thinly sliced peeled apples
 ½ cup sugar
 1½ teaspoons ground cinnamon
 14 to 16 crepes (page 37)

Melt 1 tablespoon butter or margarine in a wide frying pan; add apples, ¼ cup sugar, and ½ teaspoon cinnamon. Cover and cook on medium heat, turning apples occasionally with a wide spatula, until fruit is soft.

Spoon an equal amount of the fruit (using all) down the center of each crepe; roll to enclose filling. Arrange crepes, seam side down, side by side in a shallow baking pan or dish (about 7 by 11 inches). Sprinkle with remaining sugar and cinnamon and dot with remaining butter. (At this point you can cover and chill dish until time to heat.) Bake, uncovered, in a 350° oven for 15 minutes to heat through (20 minutes, if chilled). Makes 7 or 8 servings.

Finnish Pancake

From the western provinces of Finland comes a billowing oven pancake of eggs, butter, and milk. Honey provides the sweetness; sliced ripe peaches are the seasonal finish but you can also use frozen or canned peaches or other fruit of your choice.

 4 eggs
   About ¼ cup honey
 ½ teaspoon salt
 2½ cups milk
 1 cup all-purpose flour, unsifted
 ¼ cup (⅛ lb.) butter or margarine
 4 to 6 medium-size peaches or 4 to 6 cups
   frozen or canned peaches
 2 tablespoons lemon juice (optional)

Choose a frying pan (that can go into oven) or round baking pan or dish that is about 11 inches wide and 3 inches deep or 12 inches wide and about 2 inches deep. Put pan in 425° oven for about 10 minutes while preparing pancake batter.

In a bowl, beat together eggs, ¼ cup honey, salt, and milk. Add flour; beat until blended and smooth.

(Recipe continued on next page)

Remove pan from oven, put in butter, and stir until it melts; pour batter into hot pan. Bake for about 25 minutes or until knife inserted in center comes out clean. Meanwhile, peel peaches and mix with lemon juice to prevent darkening (omit lemon if using frozen or canned fruit). Serve pancake immediately; spoon into bowls and top with peaches and additional honey. Makes 8 to 10 servings.

Oatmeal Date Pie

A rich and tasty variation on the pecan pie theme, but made with oatmeal instead of nuts.

  ¼ cup (⅛ lb.) soft butter or margarine
  1 cup honey
  3 eggs
  ⅛ teaspoon salt
  1 teaspoon vanilla
 1¼ cups regular or quick-cooking rolled oats
  ¾ cup chopped pitted dates
  1 unbaked 9-inch pastry shell (page 92)
     Vanilla ice cream or whipped cream
       (optional)

Beat butter and honey together until fluffy; add eggs and beat until smooth. Stir in salt, vanilla, oats, and dates. Pour date mixture into pastry shell. Bake in a 350° oven for 45 minutes or until center is set when lightly touched.

Let cool completely before cutting. Top each serving with ice cream or whipped cream, if you wish. Makes about 8 servings.

For individual servings without pie crust, pour the pie filling mixture into 6 greased custard cups (6-oz. size). Pour about 1 inch hot water in a 9 by 13-inch baking pan; set custard cups in the water and bake uncovered in a 325° oven for 40 minutes or until set when touched lightly. Serve warm or cold.

Winter Apple Pie

Golden Delicious apples are ideal for pie making —they are so sweet they require very little additional sugar; the slices hold their shape well; and the fruit, though moist, is not so juicy that it requires a thickening agent. Slices of cheddar cheese or scoops of ice cream are time-approved toppings for apple pie.

     Pastry for 2-crust 9-inch pie (page 92)
  8 to 10 cups peeled, cored, and sliced Golden
       Delicious apples (8 to 10 large apples)
     About ⅓ cup sugar
  1 to 2 teaspoons ground cinnamon
  2 or 3 tablespoons butter or margarine

Roll out half the pastry on a floured board; then fit into a 9-inch pie pan. Mix apples with ⅓ cup sugar and as much cinnamon as you like. Pile apples into pastry-lined pan, mounding with your hands to make fruit as compact and secure as possible. Dot with butter.

Roll out remaining pastry on floured board and cover apples with pastry. Seal and flute edges of pastry and pierce top in several places; sprinkle lightly with sugar.

Place on lowest rack in oven and bake at 375° for about 45 minutes or until crust is richly browned. (If pastry edges begin to brown too much, cover dark area with a strip of foil.) Let pie stand until just slightly warm or cooled before cutting; this gives time for apples to reabsorb any juices so the pie will cut and serve in neat pieces. (You can rewarm the pie—it will cut well; place in a 350° oven for 15 minutes.) Makes about 8 servings.

Summer Apple Pie

Gravensteins make a brief summer appearance and also a delicious pie. They are a juicy fruit, though, and require different handling than the Golden Delicious.

     Pastry for 2-crust 9-inch pie (page 92)
  ¾ cup sugar
  3 tablespoons quick-cooking tapioca, or 2½
       tablespoons cornstarch, or ¼ cup
       all-purpose flour
  1 teaspoon ground cinnamon
  ¼ teaspoon ground cardamom or ground
       ginger (optional)
  7 or 8 cups peeled, cored, and sliced Graven-
       stein apples (7 or 8 large apples)
  2 or 3 tablespoons butter or margarine

Roll out half the pastry on a floured board; then fit into a 9-inch pie pan. In a large bowl blend sugar with tapioca, cinnamon, and cardamom; then add apples and mix well. Pour apples into pastry and mound with your hands to make fruit fit securely in the pan. Dot fruit with butter.

Roll out remaining pastry on floured board and cover apples with pastry. Seal and flute edges of pastry and pierce top in several places. Place pie on lowest rack in oven. Bake at 375° for about 1 hour or until pastry is well browned and juices inside are bubbling vigorously. (If pastry edges begin to brown too much, cover dark area with a strip of foil.)

Let pie stand until just slightly warm or cooled before serving, so the pieces will cut well and the juices will thicken. (You can rewarm the pie—it will cut well; place in a 350° oven for 15 minutes.) Makes about 8 servings.

Orange raisin apple pie. Use the preceding winter or summer apple pie recipe, omitting the ground cinnamon and mixing with the apples ½ cup raisins and ¾ teaspoon grated orange peel.

Streusel apple pie. Use the preceding summer apple pie recipe with these changes: Make pastry for a single-crust 9-inch pie and flute pastry in pan to form a high rim. Decrease apple slices to 6 cups, decrease sugar to ½ cup, and use 2 tablespoons quick-cooking tapioca for thickening. Pack apple mixture into pastry shell.

For topping, combine 1⅓ cups unsifted all-purpose flour, ⅔ cup firmly packed brown sugar, ½ cup (¼ lb.) firm butter or margarine, and 1 teaspoon grated lemon peel. Rub mixture with fingers until evenly mixed; squeeze handfuls of mixture to form big lumps; then break into nuggets and scatter over apples. Bake on lowest rack in a 375° oven for about 1 hour or until crust is well browned.

in pastry. Bake in a 400° oven for 20 minutes or until center of torte is firm when gently shaken. Remove pan sides. Serve torte warm or cooled. Makes 6 to 8 servings.

Toasted almonds. Chop ½ cup blanched almonds and spread out in a shallow pan. Bake in a 325° oven for about 10 minutes or until nuts are golden; stir occasionally.

Press-in pastry. Combine 1 cup unsifted all-purpose flour, 2 tablespoons sugar, and 6 tablespoons firm butter or margarine. With your fingers rub mixture until evenly blended. With a fork stir in 1 egg yolk, mixing until dough clings together. Press dough evenly over bottoms and sides of a 9-inch cake pan with removable bottom. Bake in a 325° oven for 30 minutes or until golden; use hot or cooled.

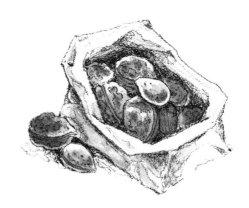

Rice Torte

From Bologna comes this delectable Italian interpretation of rice pudding.

    3 cups milk
    ¼ cup long grain rice
    ½ cup sugar
    ¼ teaspoon salt
    2 tablespoons butter or margarine
    3 eggs, slightly beaten
    ¼ teaspoon almond extract
       Toasted almonds (directions follow)
       Press-in pastry (directions follow)

Combine in the top of a double boiler the milk, rice, sugar, salt, and butter. Place over simmering water, cover, and cook, stirring occasionally, for about 2½ hours or until rice is very tender to bite.

Pour some of the hot milk into eggs, mixing; then add eggs to rice. Remove from heat, add almond extract and almonds, and pour into press-

Tofu Orange Almond Pudding

Tofu makes a surprisingly refreshing dessert when mixed with fruit syrup. To learn more about tofu, see page 79.

    ¾ to 1 pound fresh soybean pudding or soft or
       medium-firm tofu
    1 can (11 oz.) mandarin oranges, drained
    1½ teaspoons grated orange peel
    1 cup *each* sugar and fresh orange juice
    ⅛ teaspoon almond extract

Drain soybean pudding or tofu in a colander for about 30 minutes. Cut in ½-inch cubes and place in a serving bowl; add oranges.

In a small pan combine orange peel, sugar, and juice. Boil rapidly, uncovered, until reduced to 1 cup. Remove from heat, add almond extract, and pour over tofu. Cover and chill before serving. Makes 4 servings.

Spiced Mexican Custard

Cinnamon turns simple baked custard into the Mexican specialty jericalla (hari-*kah*-yah). To develop the distinctive spicy flavor, yet preserve the pale gold tones of this custard, you heat the milk and sugar with cinnamon sticks and let this mixture chill overnight. Then set the cinnamon sticks aside and bake the custards.

2 cups milk
2 sticks whole cinnamon, each 3 or 4 inches long
½ cup sugar
3 eggs, beaten

Combine milk, cinnamon sticks, and sugar in pan and bring to a boil, stirring. Cover and chill overnight.

Set 4 small baking dishes (each at least ⅔-cup

At the Bottom of It: The Crust

This dough makes a flaky, mildly flavored pastry. The trick is to keep it tender by not stretching or overhandling the dough, and to get it into the pie pan gently so it's more inclined to hold its shape if baked "blind" (empty).

A pastry cloth and a stockinet cover for your rolling pin are the best tools with which to make a good, trouble-free pastry; a wooden board on which to roll the dough is next best. You'll be much more likely to have trouble with dough sticking on a slick surface like a plastic counter —the flour on which you roll won't stay in place.

Basic Flaky Pastry

Single crust for 9-inch pie.

1⅓ cups all-purpose flour, unsifted
¼ to ⅓ teaspoon salt
⅓ cup shortening, lard, butter, or margarine
2½ to 3 tablespoons water

Double crust for 9-inch pie.

2 cups all-purpose flour, unsifted
½ teaspoon salt
½ cup shortening, lard, butter, or margarine
5 to 5½ tablespoons water

Mix flour with salt in a bowl. Add half of the shortening. Using a pastry blender or two knives, cut shortening into flour until mixture resembles cornmeal. Add remaining shortening and cut it into flour until the largest pieces are the size of small peas.

Sprinkle the water, a tablespoon at a time, over flour, tossing lightly with a fork as you add liquid. Stir vigorously in a circular motion, drawing the dough into a ball; add a little more water if mixture will not hold together. Pat into a ball. (For double-crust pie, divide dough into slightly uneven portions, using larger amount for bottom layer; cover unrolled portion.)

Dust surface of dough lightly with more flour, and with your hand, pat into a flat, round cake with smooth edges.

On a well-floured pastry cloth or board, roll out from center of dough to form a circle that extends at least 1¾ inches beyond outside rim of pie pan. (Roll top crust in the same manner, but circle need extend only 1¼ to 1½ inches beyond pan rim.) *Do not stretch* (pull) dough—always roll to make larger. If your circle of dough isn't shaping up as desired, push (do not fold) the edge back toward the center. While dough cake is still fairly small, turn over occasionally, brushing flour beneath to prevent sticking.

Fold circle of dough gently in half and lift into pie pan. Center and fit dough into pan, easing and patting in place. For single-crust pie, fold overhang under, crimp or flute edge decoratively with floured fingers, or press down with a floured fork. For double-crust pie, fill according to choice and place top crust on surface. Pinch together edges of upper and lower dough; then fold under and tuck extra dough in between edges of bottom crust and rim of pan. Crimp or flute edge firmly with floured fingers to seal, or press down gently with floured fork. Cut slits in top crust to let steam escape. Bake as directed in filled pie recipe.

To bake a single, unfilled crust, prick pastry shell liberally with tines of a fork before baking to allow steam to escape and prevent buckling of crust (check during early baking and prick any bubbles that form, so steam won't force pastry out of shape). If you have trouble making pastry stay in place, you can follow this procedure: nest a large piece of foil, edges turned up to make a pocket, in the crust, making sure foil does not cut into edges of crust. Fill with enough dry beans or rice to hold in place. This retains crust shape, but bottom does not brown as much as the rim. Bake in a 350° oven for 16 to 18 minutes or until golden brown. Fill as desired.

size) in a baking pan and surround with hottest tap water to about half the depth of the dishes. Remove dishes, set the pan of water in the oven, and set heat at 350°. When oven has reached that temperature, reheat the milk mixture to scalding, stirring. Set cinnamon aside and beat hot milk into the eggs with a fork. Pour an equal portion of mixture into each baking dish and set the dishes in the hot-water bath.

Bake at 350° for 25 to 30 minutes or until the centers of the custards jiggle only slightly when a dish is shaken gently. Remove custards from water at once, using a wide spatula or kitchen tongs. Chill custards and serve in the baking dishes. If you like, rinse cinnamon sticks, drain, and break in halves. Set a piece atop each jericalla. Makes 4 servings.

Nockerln

A golden cloud of hot nockerln accented by fluffs of cold whipped cream, all strewn with melting bits of semisweet chocolate, is a totally luxurious dessert that belies its simplicity—and ease.

Nockerln are just eggs, separated—yolks and whites are whipped with a little sugar and flour to airy lightness, then folded back together and baked in a little butter.

You can have everything organized, with whipped cream and grated chocolate in the refrigerator, and then make the nockerln right after dinner; they cook in about 5 minutes.

  4 eggs, separated
  4 tablespoons sugar
  4 teaspoons all-purpose flour
  2 tablespoons butter or margarine
  1 cup whipping cream, whipped and sweetened
       to taste
     About ½ cup grated semisweet chocolate

With an electric mixer at high speed, beat whites until soft peaks form; then gradually add sugar and continue to whip until stiff peaks form. Set aside. With the same beater (unwashed), whip yolks until they are about doubled in volume; add flour and continue to beat until very thick. Gently fold yolks into whites.

Melt butter in a shallow oval 1½-quart baking pan over direct heat; when butter is just beginning to brown, spoon mounds of egg mixture into pan.

Place at once in a 350° oven and bake for 5 to 8 minutes, just until nockerln are tinged golden brown. They should still be semiliquid in center;

if baked firm, flavor is less delicate.

Spoon at once onto dessert plates and top with whipped cream and grated chocolate. Makes 4 or 5 servings.

Whole Wheat Carrot Cake

Carrots are the special ingredient in this wholesome cake. Finely shredded into the batter, they lose their identity in baking but are vital in contributing a nutritious moistness. Try making the cake with chocolate (directions follow).

  2 eggs
  ⅔ cup salad oil
  1 cup firmly packed brown sugar
  1 cup whole wheat flour
1½ teaspoons soda
  1 teaspoon ground cinnamon
  ½ teaspoon salt
  1 cup grated or finely shredded carrots
       (about 1½ large carrots)
     Cream cheese frosting (recipe follows)

In a bowl, beat eggs just until blended; add oil and sugar; beat until thoroughly mixed. Stir together flour, soda, cinnamon, and salt. Stir into egg mixture just until blended; add carrots. Pour into greased 8-inch-square pan.

Bake in a 350° oven for 30 to 35 minutes or until a wooden pick inserted in center comes out clean. Let cool in pan on rack. When cool, spread cream cheese frosting evenly over top. Makes 9 servings.

Cream cheese frosting. In a small bowl, blend smoothly 1½ ounces (half of a 3-oz. package) cream cheese and ¼ cup (⅛ lb.) soft butter or margarine. Add 2 cups sifted powdered sugar and ½ teaspoon *each* grated orange peel and vanilla; beat until creamy.

Whole wheat chocolate carrot cake. Follow preceding recipe, but omit ground cinnamon. Melt 2 ounces semisweet chocolate and add, along with 1 teaspoon vanilla, to egg mixture.

Accessible Zest

The grated peel or zest of oranges and lemons is a useful flavoring element that you can keep on hand in the freezer. For example, next time you are juicing oranges, grate the peel first, spread it out in a shallow pan, and freeze. Then break up the bits of frozen peel and store in a plastic bag, to measure out as needed.

Index

Tips on Thrift

Shopping Guides

Storage Techniques

Thrifty Kitchen